OAKVILLE'S FLOWER

OAKVILLE'S FLOWER

THE HISTORY OF HMCS *OAKVILLE*

SEAN E. LIVINGSTON

DUNDURN

TORONTO

Project Editor: Jennifer McKnight
Copy Editor: Britanie Wilson
Design: Laura Boyle
Printer: Webcom
Cover Design: Courtney Horner
Front and Back Cover Image: Courtesy of Edward Stewart

Library and Archives Canada Cataloguing in Publication

Livingston, Sean E., author
    Oakville's flower : the history of HMCS Oakville / Sean E. Livingston.

Includes bibliographical references and index.
Issued in print and electronic formats.
ISBN 978-1-4597-2841-7 (pbk.).--ISBN 978-1-4597-2842-4 (pdf).--
ISBN 978-1-4597-2843-1 (epub)

    1. Oakville (Corvette). 2. Corvettes (Warships)--Canada--History--20th century. 3. World War, 1939-1945--Naval operations, Canadian. 4. World War, 1939-1945--Campaigns--Atlantic Ocean. 5. Canada. Royal Canadian Navy--History--World War, 939-1945. I. Title.

VA400.5.O46L59 2014   359.3'2540971   C2014-904983-8
                                                           C2014-904984-6

1 2 3 4 5   18 17 16 15 14

We acknowledge the support of the **Canada Council for the Arts** and the **Ontario Arts Council** for our publishing program. We also acknowledge the financial support of the **Government of Canada** through the **Canada Book Fund** and **Livres Canada Books**, and the **Government of Ontario** through the **Ontario Book Publishing Tax Credit** and the **Ontario Media Development Corporation.**

Care has been taken to trace the ownership of copyright material used in this book. The author and the publisher welcome any information enabling them to rectify any references or credits in subsequent editions.

J. Kirk Howard, President

The publisher is not responsible for websites or their content unless they are owned by the publisher.

Printed and bound in Canada.

VISIT US AT
Dundurn.com | *@dundurnpress* | *Facebook.com/dundurnpress* | *Pinterest.com/dundurnpress*

Dundurn
3 Church Street, Suite 500
Toronto, Ontario, Canada
M5E 1M2

Dedicated in memory of Anna Stewart,
Late wife of Edward Stewart;
And to all those sailors who served aboard HMCS Oakville.

CONTENTS

ACKNOWLEDGEMENTS

As with any historical work there are several people who have generously devoted their time and resources to help me bring the history of HMCS *Oakville* to the public. I would be amiss if I didn't recognize the man who got me "hooked" on the history of the ship in the first place: Edward (Ed) Stewart. Ed is an accomplished naval historian and for years has hunted down and collected various bits of information regarding the ship, including the lion-share of images presented in this book. He's been a source of constant support, guidance, and wisdom, and his commitment to preserving and sharing our community's naval heritage is laudable. For over a decade Ed has been as good a friend and colleague as one could ever hope for on such a journey, and for that he has my sincere thanks.

I also have to acknowledge the work done by Adrial Fitzgerald — friend, scholar, and one of the few people willing to take the time out of a busy schedule to edit early drafts of my manuscript. His feedback, respectful criticisms, and unwavering support have been invaluable. Make no mistake, good sir; asking a friend to meticulously go through a manuscript is no small request and you never — not once — made me feel like a burden. *Gratias tibi ago.*

Carolyn Cross and Susan Semeczko of the Oakville Museum are wonderful people who have supported me since the first museum exhibit I ran with Ed. Their passion for local history and willingness to support me at every turn has been deeply appreciated. Your belief in me and in my labours has been so touching: I will never forget the day I walked into the museum to see my research and words stenciled on the walls. Every time I visit, your excitement and encouragement has been infectious, and no matter how many times I ask for assistance — be it pictures or information related to our local history — you've always been more than happy to help. I should note that in the last days of working on this book, Carolyn provided me with some important information that greatly contributed to *Oakville's* history. You have always believed in the importance of telling the story of HMCS *Oakville*, and without your support it would have never gained the momentum it has in the community.

Lieutenant (Navy) Bryan McIntyre CD has served with RCSCC *Oakville* since its formation, and has been a true supporter of the corps and its history since the beginning. In fact, he's the longest serving officer with RCSCC *Oakville*. When I asked him to help me in canvassing the local community to support this work, he not only jumped at the chance, but went above and beyond. I couldn't have done it without your help — you have been a good friend, comrade, and shipmate. Cheers!

Additionally, the Oakville Navy League has stood behind this project from the start, fulfilling the ambitions of one of its first presidents, Linda Gignac. I think she would be proud to see that the history of the corps and its namesake ship has made it into a book. I'd also like to thank Henry Lach, our league liaison, who ensured the slew of images in this book were copied and converted into the correct format required by the printers. Thank you so much for taking the time out of your hectic schedule to ensure these images made it into the book.

I'm also indebted to Jack Russell and his family for their kind support and enthusiasm regarding the history of HMCS *Oakville*. Jack was always willing to chat with me regarding his time aboard *Oakville*, and no matter how many times I called, no matter how many questions I asked, he was more than happy to do what he could to help. His kind donation of artifacts to the Oakville Museum is a reflection of his generous spirit. Thanks for the tales and for the laughs — this book is as much for you as it is for all your shipmates.

I'd also like to thank Beth Bruder, Vice-President of Dundurn Press Limited, for her belief in this project and patience in answering my many questions. Carrie Gleason, Managing Editor, and Jaclyn Hodsdon, Publicist, were both very helpful in assisting a new author with the ins-and-outs of preparing and promoting a manuscript. Lastly, I feel very fortunate to have Jennifer McKnight and Britanie Wilson as my editors and am grateful for all of their work and assistance on this book.

Thanks are extended to Lieutenant-Commander (LCdr) Glenn Woolfrey MMM, CD for his leadership and steadfast support in preserving the history of HMCS *Oakville* at every turn. His efforts and generosity were key in promoting this book within the Royal Canadian Navy (RCN) and the local community. Additionally, I'd like to express my gratitude to Captain Arjeh van der Sluis SBStJ CD; Mike Vencel; Lieutenant (Navy) (Lt(N)) Walter Dermott CD; Captain Mark Philips; Adam Everingham; Lt(N) Shane Crawford SBStJ, CD; and Lt(N) Lou Taddeo SBStJ, CD for the various ways they assisted in supporting the creation of this book and preserving the memory of Oakville's naval past.

I would also like to recognize the volunteers at the Oakville Historical Society for their assistance with researching both this work and my previous paper on the christening of HMCS *Oakville*. They were more than happy to help a young researcher find the necessary bits of history he was searching for.

Special thanks to H.E. "The Chevalier" Stephen Lautens GCJ, Grand Master of The Order of St. Joachim, as well as to my fellow Knights and Dames, for their assistance and fraternal support throughout this endeavor — *JUNXIT AMICUS AMOR*.

Special thanks are also extended to my good friend Michael Penney for his years of friendship and encouragement. He is the brother I never had, and in many ways kindled my desire to write. You are the most creative and talented person I know and I look forward to your many future successes!

So much of this would not have been possible without the support of a truly wonderful woman, Trish Feil, who, when I needed it the most, gave me the nudge or kick in the butt that kept me going with this project. Trish, you were always willing to hear me read — and reread — passages of this book and give me honest feedback, but most touching of all, you never once faltered in your belief in me. I'm so happy to have shared this part of my life with you, which has made it all the more rewarding.

Naturally, a great debt of gratitude is owed to my parents, Edward and Gisele Livingston. If not for their lifelong encouragement, I would not be the man I am today. Thank you both for your guidance and love. No matter the endeavour — be it joining the Canadian Armed Forces at the age of 17 (which required parental consent — my mother was, shall we say, a bit nervous signing the documents) or writing this book — you have always believed and supported me.

And, perhaps most importantly, my sincere and humble thanks to the crew of HMCS *Oakville* — all the veterans who made an effort to contact the league, Ed, and myself over the years to share their stories, donate items and pictures, and help unlock the story of the famous corvette. This is your story and legacy, and I have been honoured to be the one to share it. Ready Aye Ready.

PREFACE
Discovering "*Oakville*"

When I teach history, either in high school or the cadet corps, I find it necessary to first define what this thing called *history* exactly is. Ultimately it is the study of the human race through various sources (pictorial, written, audio-visual, etc.), but my focus is primarily to ensure that they understand that being a student of history requires great care. Aside from researching, scrutinizing sources, and detecting author bias, I tell my pupils and cadets that it is important to appreciate the fragility of history — it can easily be lost. Simply forego documenting an event or life — put nothing to paper, take no visual images, lose or destroy documentation — and it fades away as if never there. And losing history can have grave consequences.

The historian well knows that history is delicate. Frequently, and especially with the passage of time, the past leaves us only with faint clues, fragments of evidence that require historians to become keen detectives. In analyzing these, one can easily make mistakes, and just as the detective fears making a false accusation based on a poorly executed investigation, so too the historian fears drawing false conclusions based on misinterpreted sources. Thus, the chief point I clarify for my students is this: as students of history (and who among us isn't, really?), they are each *keepers* of historical knowledge and must fulfill the dual role of researcher *and* guardian. Put simply, they are to *objectively* study and reconstruct the past, not only for the pursuit of their own knowledge, but to ensure that they prevent its loss by passing it down as accurately as possible to successive generations.

Studying history is both natural and unavoidable. We all have a desire to know our past, and as history teachers we love to preach: without this knowledge we are doomed to repeat the mistakes of previous generations. Preserving our past and avoiding such doom is the primary reason for this publication.

My involvement with HMCS* *Oakville* began over 12 years ago. My father was a friend of Commander R.K. (Bob) Bonnell CD, who was the commanding officer of HMCS *York*, a naval reserve unit in Toronto. Bob invited him to attend a parade, and my father took me along. I was in high school at the time, and remember being enthralled by the uniforms and ceremony. Afterwards, I was invited to the various messes and was greeted warmly. The members took kindly to my inquisitive nature, answering my questions and sharing bits of naval history with me. At the end of the evening, I recall Bob

* His/Her Majesty's Canadian Ship

joking that they would suit me up with a uniform and press-gang me into the service. A year later, at only 17, I joined as a boatswain (at that age it was necessary to receive my parents' consent).

Over the years, as I began and progressed through my undergraduate studies, I realized that I wanted to pursue a career in education and started exploring ways to become more involved in adolescent education. It was suggested by someone at *York* that I should work with the Sea Cadets to gain experience for my application to teachers' college. I decided to take the advice and began volunteering. Not long afterwards, I started the process of transferring from the Primary Naval Reserve to the Cadet Instructor Cadre, a branch of the Canadian Armed Forces made up of commissioned officers whose role it is to instruct cadets (see chapter 6 for more details on cadets).

During this time I had my first meeting with HMCS *Oakville*. I was taking a course at the University of Toronto on Canadian History, and as a naval reservist, resolved on the incredibly ambitious and slightly presumptuous task of writing a culminating essay on the Canadian navy in the Second World War. In researching, I came across a ship that shared the same name of the town I lived in — *Oakville* — and briefly made note of it in my essay.

My next encounter occurred when I joined Royal Canadian Sea Cadet Corps 178 Oakville and met local naval historian Edward (Ed) Stewart. The corps was young, only a few years old, and he had been one of the principal people behind its formation. I learned that its name, number, and crest came directly from the warship I had come across in my studies. As we spoke and developed a friendship over the years, I became more and more interested in the story of this ship. Although I wasn't fully aware of it at the time, Ed was the main person keeping the fragile history of this ship alive, and through him I became drawn into its history.

I awoke to just how delicate this history was during my final year of undergraduate studies. I was taking a fourth-year seminar on "Spectacle, Crowds, and Parades" in Canada and needed to choose a Canadian event to research for an essay. Upon mentioning it to Ed, he suggested writing on the christening ceremony of HMCS *Oakville*, which had occurred in the town of Oakville itself. I visited the local historical society and museum to begin my research and was both amazed and alarmed. Although many photos of the ceremony had survived and were in excellent condition, they were without captions and explanation, leaving me confused as to what was happening in the images, where they had taken place, who appeared in them, and what their chronological order was in relation to one another. Aside from a ship's synopsis, the ceremony programme, and a brief eyewitness account, local records regarding *Oakville's* christening were non-existent. To make matters worse, the local newspaper archive was missing editions from the period. I continued my search at Robarts Library at the University of Toronto, where I had access to microfiche newspaper sources. What I discovered absolutely floored me.

Major newspapers such as the *Toronto Daily Star*, *Toronto Evening Telegram*, the *Globe and Mail*, and the *Hamilton Spectator* had covered the event in detail, assigning it front-page coverage. The event even attracted international media, and was reported in the *New York* and *London Times*. A wealth of information and coverage on the spectacle had emerged, allowing me not only to explain what happened that day, but also provide substance to the town archive photos. It quickly became clear that not only was this event the largest spectacle that the town of Oakville had ever had, but that it was one of the largest, if not the largest, christening ceremony of a Canadian naval ship during the Second World War! What I couldn't understand was how something so pivotal to the town's history had been almost completely forgotten. Ironically, even the mayor at the time boasted that the ceremony was "one to be remembered."[1]

I no longer was writing for my course — I was doing it out of necessity, to keep this history from being lost. The essay, "Oakville's Forgotten Fame — A Rediscovery of the Christening of HMCS Oakville, 1941," drew the interest of the town's historical and cultural department, and was entered into the main library's reference section. Shortly thereafter I assisted Ed, who was creating an exhibit dedicated to HMCS *Oakville* at the town museum. On the opening night,

I gave a speech on my essay to a full crowd and later assisted with walkthroughs. The event, which ran over a month, was a great success. As the museum's caretaker simply declared, it was the first time she'd ever seen a line up out the door to see an exhibit. We had struck a nerve with the community, and I had become fully immersed in the history of this warship.

It was sometime later that Ed said something to me that started me on the path to writing this book. One evening he made a comment that stuck with me: "Well kid, it's all you now." Confused at the meaning behind this statement, I asked him to clarify. "*Oakville*," he said, "the history of the ship! It's on your shoulders now." No one alive knew more about the ship than me, and Ed wasn't a writer and was getting older. If anyone was going to ensure that the memory of this ship would not be forgotten, it would have to be me. *I* had to tell its tale.

The story of HMCS *Oakville* has never been fully told. Pieces appear here and there, but no definitive, exclusive publication on the ship has ever been created. This is somewhat surprising considering the history of HMCS *Oakville* possesses passion, adventure and heroism — all ingredients that make its story well suited for a novel. It touches lives, a community, and a country, and like many great stories, its ending is one of faded glory and ill-fated demise. Yet the story of HMCS *Oakville* is not fiction — it is about real Canadians and real events during some of our country's darkest times. In May 2010, the Canadian navy celebrated its centennial anniversary, a hundred years of faithful service.

There is no better time for the story of one of its most distinguished ships and crews to come to light.

Writing this novel, however, is a matter of personal obligation and conscience. The consequence of not telling this story would be wounding, not only for the community of Oakville, whose history is so intertwined with that of this warship, but also for the country as a whole. HMCS *Oakville*'s story is one that all Canadians should be proud of, and the actions of those brave Canadian sailors who sailed her should never be forgotten. I was obliged to undertake this endeavour because failing to do so would be to keep this history hidden, where it may easily have slipped from the annals of time. Out of necessity, I switch from researcher to guardian, to preserve this great story and give it due recognition. I write it for those brave veterans who risked life and limb for Canada — the crew of HMCS *Oakville* who did their part to protect our country and secure victory for the allies. Our part is to remember them — remember their actions and what they were willing to sacrifice for all of us. A simple phrase remains at the forefront of my conscience: "Lest we forget."

Ed and I have striven to compile a complete history of HMCS *Oakville*, not just of its meritorious actions in war, but of its whole history: how it touched and provided hope for a community (if not the whole country) and how its memory lives on presently in the town after which it is named. I therefore humbly submit our labours, trusting that you'll find *Oakville*'s story as fascinating, insightful, and moving as we have.

Yours aye,

Sean E. Livingston SBStJ, CD
Lieutenant (Navy)

CHAPTER 1
Cheap and Nasty

THE COMING CONFLICT

War was in the air during the waning years of the 1930s. While Canada struggled to overcome an economic depression, across the seas Nazi Germany was gearing up for conquest. Although Canadians could see the storm gathering in the distance, there was little enthusiasm for the possible conflict to come. The memory of the First World War was still fresh in people's minds — the wounds and scars still haunting those who had heeded the call for "king and country." Fathers had little desire to see their sons off to a war that threatened to be more potent and brutal than the one they had fought nearly two decades ago. In that conflict they had lost their innocence — a naïve and adventurous spirit that had rushed them overseas to heroically fight in a war that would be over before Christmas. Years in the muddy trenches of Europe, surrounded by death, blood, and daily hardship, had long taken away such romantic illusions.

Likewise, Canada was far from ready to fight another war. After the First World War, Canada took a financially conservative approach to military planning. Throughout the 1920s and 1930s it cut defence spend-ing, focusing more on domestic issues than foreign affairs. Though Prime Minister William Lyon Mackenzie King realized the coming danger, he was slow to act, knowing that another war with Germany was the last thing Canadians wanted. As he wrote in his diary, "No sacrifice can be too great which can save a war."[1]

By 1939, the decades of neglect had taken their toll. Canada's military had been weakened to the point that it could no longer defend its own coasts, let alone muster a fully trained and equipped expeditionary force to be sent overseas. The permanent army had just over 4,000 officers and partially trained men, armed with little to no modern military equipment. The air force only had roughly 50 modern aircraft, and the Canadian navy fewer than a dozen fighting ships. Although it was severely lacking in military resources, Canada did have a well-devised mobilization plan that, when the time came, would greatly assist in generating an overseas combat force.

Canada was not alone in its anti-war sentiments. Former allies, such as Britain, France, and the United States, also resisted the notion of fighting another costly war. Britain was still far from having recovered from the effects of the First World War when it was struck by the Great Depression; France, despite its greater self-sufficiency, still suffered hardships, unemployment, and civil unrest; and the United States, whose stock market crash served as the catalyst to the global economic downturn, had passed Neutrality Acts to prevent being drawn into another war. Britain and France, in a bid to secure peace, had further adopted a policy of "appeasement" towards Nazi Germany, and in tow, Canada followed their lead. Economically and emotionally, this was a fight many wanted to avoid.

However, try as they may to avoid it, the foundation of this coming conflict was set nearly 20 years earlier. It was a strong foundation, hardened by Germany's bitter sense of being unjustly punished by the peace agreement of the First World War — the Treaty of Versailles. Drawn six months after the armistice by the victors of the war, it contained some 440 articles that Germany had to accept. Its conditions were harsh, designed to cripple the country so that it could never again pose a threat to peace in Europe. Article 231, the infamous "War Guilt Clause," assigned sole blame and responsibility for the war to Germany. It was to be held accountable for any damage inflicted on Allied civilian populations and would have to pay those countries reparations, which left the German economy in tatters. The treaty also imposed restrictions on Germany's military. It was limited to a maximum of 100,000 men, and weapons such as heavy artillery, gas, tanks, and aircraft were banned. The navy was not to surpass 10,000 tons and submarines were strictly prohibited. Defeated, humiliated, and feeling unjustly punished, the German people would be vulnerable to right-wing extremists who promised a return to greatness.

Adolf Hitler and his National Socialist German Workers Party ("Nazi" for short) would profit from this national disparity. He rose to power, and from his election as Chancellor of Germany in 1933, ushered in sweeping economic and political reform. Creating a totalitarian government, he snubbed the despised Treaty of Versailles and set on rebuilding the German military. By the late 1930s, it had grown into one of the largest and most technologically advanced fighting forces the world had ever seen. Fuelled by a contrived sense of racial superiority, the Nazi war machine was ready to go on the offensive. Striking first at the Rhine-

land, Hitler made successive expansions into Austria and Czechoslovakia. Britain and France attempted to appease him, but drew the line at Poland. There was no stopping him, though — no stopping what had started the day Germany was made to sign the Treaty of Versailles. The same document that had given birth to the League of Nations, the forerunner to the United Nations, would also seal its demise. From the smouldering ashes of the First World War would arise the flames of the Second World War, and with it a more fierce and modern kind of warfare that would plunge the world into a global conflict of epic proportion.

WAR AND NAVAL SUPREMACY

On September 1, 1939, German forces invaded Poland. Two days later, Britain and France declared war. The storm that many Canadians had been watching grow over the years had finally arrived. Although Canadians did not have an appetite for war, when the call came, the answer was again "Ready Aye Ready." Mackenzie King hastily recalled the Canadian Parliament for an emergency vote on the issue, and a nearly unanimous resolution was made. On September 10, Canada formally made its own declaration of war on Germany, and, unlike the First World War, it was truly an independent decision. Although loyalist feelings of kinship between Britain and English Canada strongly motivated the decision, a major and often overlooked motive for declaring war was self-serving: at the time, 63 percent of Canadian export trade and 39 percent of import trade was moved by the seas. The Canadian economy, largely dependent on sea trade, needed the oceans of the world to remain in friendly hands, lest its trade industry come to a damaging halt.[2]

With a declaration of war, the Canadian military now had to confront an enemy that was equipped with the latest in military technology. The Germans had an arsenal that included new aircraft, vehicles, tanks, and naval vessels. Britain was particularly concerned with the threat posed by the new German navy, the *Kriegsmarine*. As an island, it had good reason to be worried. Armed with quick and heavily fortified pocket battleships and stealthy U-boats, the German navy posed a real threat to English security. After Hitler took France, the British Isles became nearly surrounded, with the enemy facing them across the English Channel, North Sea, and part of the North Atlantic. With an invasion imminent, Britain would depend heavily on Allied supplies, which could only be transported and received by sea. Also, after Germany attacked Russia, it became even more apparent to the Allies that the only way to win the war would be to launch an offensive from Britain herself — a move that would certainly require more soldiers, food, and equipment be shipped across the Atlantic. It did not take long to see the growing importance of these seagoing supply lines. As Admiral of the Fleet, Sir Dudley Pound conceded: "If we lose the war at sea we lose the war."[3]

The Germans were keenly aware of the importance of naval supremacy for securing victory. At the outset of the war, Britain was its nearest threat; success against such an enemy would require Germany to pit itself against the famed British Royal Navy (RN), the largest and most feared navy in the world. The Germans knew that the key to defeating Britain was to starve it into submission: sever its chain of supplies. It was just like cutting off the supply of fuel to an engine. Without receiving constant shipments of critical supplies, such as food and munitions, Britain's "engine" of war — its defiant resistance to Nazi Germany — would collapse.

The U-boat was specially designed for this purpose. The name "U-boat" is the Anglicization of the word *U-boot*, itself an abbreviation of the German *Unterseeboot*, meaning "under sea boat." Well-armed and possessing quick surface speed, long-range capabilities, and manoeuvrability, submarines had the advantage of being virtually undetectable to surface vessels, enabling them to sneak unobserved, spring up, attack, and submerge before being spotted. A U-boat was essentially a torpedo-launching platform, which the Germans considered a "torpedo boat" rather than a true submarine due to its underwater limitations (hence its name). When submerged and running on electric power its speed and range were severely diminished. As a result, U-boats had to spend most of their time on the surface running on diesel engines, submerging only in defence and during rare daytime attacks. Although they tactically had the potential to be an awesome weapon against enemy surface warships, they were intended to wage an economic form of warfare by creating a naval blockade against enemy shipping. Hitler's personal order to Admiral Karl Doenitz, head of the German submarine command, made this chillingly clear: "Merchant shipping will be sunk without warning with the intention of killing as many of the crew as possible … U-boats are to surface after torpedoing and shoot up the lifeboats."[4] The complete and utter control of Western Europe rested on the Nazis' ability to waylay Trans-Atlantic merchant shipping.

U-boats had proved a formidable weapon against Allied shipping in the First World War, which was the primary reason why their construction was forbidden by the Treaty of Versailles. Yet, despite this restriction, Germany went ahead and covertly established a submarine design office in Holland and a torpedo research program in Sweden. Prior to the start of the Second World War, Germany had already begun to construct U-boats and train sailors to crew them. When discovered, Britain attempted the diplomatic "appeasement" route and came to an agreement with Germany to regulate the size of the *Kriegsmarine* in relation to the RN. The Anglo-German Naval Agreement, as it was known, allowed Germany to build a navy beyond the limits set by the Treaty of Versailles, but it was to adhere to a tonnage ratio of 35:100 in relation to the RN. Specifically regarding submarines, the agreement declared:

> In the matter of submarines, however, Germany, while not exceeding the ratio of 35:100 in respect of total tonnage, shall have the right to possess a submarine tonnage equal to the total submarine tonnage possessed by the Members of the British Commonwealth of Nations.[5]

The agreement sanctioned Germany's creation of U-boats, the stipulation being that they could not surpass the total amount of submarines in the RN. When the war started, Germany would already have 65 U-boats in its fleet, with 21 at sea ready for war.

Although the British and Canadian Admiralty knew the importance of protecting the overseas transport of vital war supplies, they mistakenly underestimated the threat posed by U-boats, concerning themselves more with the battleships and cruisers of the German surface fleet. They wrongly believed that the development of ASDIC*, or sonar, would render submarines completely vulnerable if they chose to attack shipping aggressively.[6] It took a tragedy — the sinking of SS *Athenia* — to change their views. An unarmed civilian passenger ship carrying over 1,000 non-combatants, it was sunk just hours after Britain had declared war. The perpetrator was U-boat U30, which had mistaken *Athenia* for an armed merchant cruiser. It was the first British ship sunk by the Germans in the Second World War. Stewardess Hannah Baird, a native from Montreal, was killed in the attack and would be Canada's first casualty of the war. The British First Sea Lord saw the event as a sign that Germany intended to wage unrestricted submarine warfare. Immediately the authority's views on naval warfare changed. The focus now shifted from surface warfare to combating the U-boats that would prey mercilessly on defenceless merchant vessels.[7]

Despite the shock from the sinking of *Athenia*, the first year of the war seemed to confirm pre-war beliefs regarding the threat of U-boats, but not because of an Allied strategic presence. The *Kriegsmarine* had only a small number of submarines at the outset of the war, and few with the range required for operations in the Atlantic. However, the fall of France in the summer of 1940 saw the growth of the U-boat fleet. With access to new French ports, the time required for U-boats to reach Allied shipping routes was greatly reduced.

U-boats were extremely effective in destroying Allied shipping, especially during the war's early stages. It was "*die glucliche zeit*" — "the happy time" — for German submariners, before the development of effective antisubmarine warfare. The fight against the U-boat would last the entire war and would be the focus of combat in the Atlantic. Germany had the largest submarine fleet in the Second World War and would be responsible for sinking almost 3,000 Allied ships. They were an enemy to be reckoned with, formidable in their own right. British Prime Minister Sir Winston Churchill admitted that "The only thing that ever really frightened me during the war was the U-Boat peril."[8] Ironically, the nation that would answer this threat better than any would be one whose navy at the outset of the war consisted of no more than six destroyers, five minesweepers, and two small training vessels — the Royal Canadian Navy (RCN).[9]

THE BATTLE OF THE ATLANTIC AND THE "SHEEP DOG" NAVY

After the "*Athenia* incident," the Allied response was to protect the merchant vessels by organizing them into convoys escorted by naval warships. Originating in the First World War, the RN had introduced the convoy system to defeat U-boats. It involved a group of merchant ships sailing together, surrounded by a guard of warships. U-boats found it difficult to find an isolated target, and it was hard to attack a convoy without provoking a counter-attack by its escorts.

In response to the convoy system, the Germans employed a tactic whose conception similarly dated back to the First World War: the *Rudeltaktik* or "Wolfpack." It involved forming a group of U-boats to attack a convoy en mass, rather than individually. It would overwhelm and confuse the convoy escorts; captains would not know where to direct their vessels, as the attacks would come from every direction. Each wolfpack had a "shadower" whose role was to maintain contact with the convoy and make regular reports on its position. It would remain out of sight, submerging often by day and travelling on the surface under cover

---

* ASDIC — An early form of sonar used to detect submarines. The word "ASDIC" is difficult to define. Unlike the word "sonar," which was originally an acronym for "Sound Navigation And Ranging," ASDIC is not an acronym. The British Admiralty made up the story that it stood for "Allied Submarine Detection Investigation Committee" (which many still believe it stands for). At best, ASDIC was a combination of "ASD'ics" (derived from the name of the early work: "supersonics") and "ASD'iv-ite" (which referred to the quartz piezoelectric crystals utilized by the device). ASD might have stood for Anti-Submarine Detection, with the "ic" being taken from "sonic."

RCN Corvettes in Halifax. (*Courtesy David Francis Stewart.*)

of darkness. Its small silhouette made it very difficult to detect in poor light and kept the vessel safe. Once the pack was amassed, they would attack by night and withdraw a safe distance by day, repeating the process like wolves feasting on a defenceless herd of sheep.

At the outset of the war, the RCN wasted no time assisting Britain by providing naval escorts for merchant ships. On September 16, 1939, two Canadian destroyers, *Saguenay* and *St. Laurent*, had already preformed escort duties, accompanying convoy HX1 (Halifax to United Kingdom) from Halifax 350 miles across the Atlantic, where it was transferred to the care of the RN.[10] Then, in October, Canadian destroyers again preformed a similar escort for the First Canadian Division. At this point, with limited naval assets, the role of the RCN had not yet expanded beyond the defence of its own shores.

However, the Canadian government did have a plan to create a more substantial fleet, with a focus on both the Tribal-class destroyer (as an anti-submarine vessel) and Halcyon-class minesweeper.[11] This plan had actually taken effect in May 1939, under the guidance of Mackenzie King's liberal government. As

the war loomed on the horizon, he saw the RCN as a "… marvellous vehicle for contributing to imperial security without having to send thousands of troops overseas again."[12] He believed that in the event of war, a large navy could possibly keep Canada from direct involvement in the conflict. He was more focused on the defence of Canada itself, and his government favoured naval and air force expansion in its pre-war policy. Mackenzie King knew the threat posed by the *Kriegsmarine*. Unlike in the previous World War, the danger of modern submarines, coupled with Germany's desire to establish a base in Iceland, meant that Canada could come under attack.[13]

By the end of December, the RCN had grown from 13 to 60 vessels, including destroyers, armed merchant ships, converted luxury yachts, and fishing boats.[14] Although the government had a ship-building plan, it faced immediate difficulties: Canadian yards simply did not have the expertise to build to naval standard. The answer to this problem came with the Flower-class corvette.

The corvette's name is attributed to Winston Churchill, who, as First Lord of the Admiralty at the

Port Side of HMCS *Oakville* in the Caribbean, prior to August 1942. (*Courtesy Edward Stewart.*)

outbreak of the war, decided to name the ships after flowers.[15] Canada, on the advice of the Chief of Naval Staff, Rear-Admiral Percy Nelles, chose to name them after towns instead. He felt that doing so would inspire public support, a move that would later prove its merits in the town of Oakville.

Although not the minesweeper initially desired by the RCN, the small and lightly armed corvette was very manoeuvrable and well suited for patrol and convoy escort duties. It was the brainchild of British naval designer William Reed, who designed the ship based on the Smith's Dock Company single-shaft whale-catcher, the *Southern Pride*. Its simple design, based on mercantile standards, made it easy for these small yards to rapidly produce. They were also larger than, and nearly as fast as, the Halcyon minesweepers, and needed only half the crew.[16]

Choosing a ship made to commercial standards came with consequences. Corvettes did not have any back-ups for their crucial systems and were notorious for their terrible living conditions. They were "wet" ships, due to their short fo'c'sle* that ended shy of the bridge (later designs would extended the fo'c'sle).

Seawater would continually penetrate the hull at the seams, hatches, and ventilation units during foul weather, and, as one sailor recalled, "The ship was a floating pigpen of stink. You couldn't get away from it. The butter tasted of it … the bread smelled of feet and armpits."[17] David Francis Stewart noted, "you were wet — everything was wet,"[18] and that the driest part of the ship was the boiler room**

These woes were further exacerbated by the ships' "lively" nature — they had a tendency to roll easily, a by-product of their whaler design. This problem was so evident that sailors would commonly joke that they would even "roll on wet grass." Stewart remembered how quickly the motion of the ship made sailors ill: "just before you get out of the harbour, you get that Atlantic swell and, bam, I got sick!" As he explained: "It's not the rolling that got you — it's the whole god-damn up-and-down."[19] C.J. McDonald, a seaman aboard HMCS *Oakville* from 1943 to 1944, summarized the experience: "I was sick all the time at sea. I enjoyed being out at sea, except for the seasickness — a hell of a lot worse than a hangover."[20] His shipmate, Jack Russell, who served in HMCS *Oakville* from 1943 to 1945, recalled similar challenges being in a corvette: "I was seasick for

* Derived from the word "forecastle," fo'c'sle refers to the forward part of a ship directly below the deck, which traditionally was used to store equipment or serve as the crew's living quarters.

** As a signalman, Stewart had occasion to head down to the ship's boilers to burn confidential papers.

2–3 days,"[21] he said during an interview, and from his tone, it was evident that the experience was miserable. The first few days at sea went by like a blur for Russell: "We stayed close to shore going down the Atlantic sea coast. I didn't care where the ship went because I was so seasick."[22] By the time they made it to Florida, Russell was fortunate enough to have finally earned his sea legs. He remembered, "… that's when I finally became a first class sailor."[23] After that, he was never sick again while at sea, the ship and chop having "worked it out of him."[24]

Poor weather only made conditions worse. Stewart recalled one instance when his ship came off the coast of west Ireland and was blindsided by a storm while en route to a convoy:

> You would come up on a wave and you could see everything for miles it lifted you so high into the air. Then you'd come down, like you were riding down a slide at an [amusement] park, and it would be just like a giant bucket of water being poured on top of you. You'd have water in your boots. We were wet going in and coming out.[25]

He recalled the Officer of the Watch (OOW) stating, "well boys, that had to be a seventy-five footer!"[26] When navigating in large swells, it was as if "you were in a valley between green mountains of water — a beautiful green — and you couldn't see anything beyond them."[27] As a signalman, Stewart's post on a corvette was on the bridge, which was open and exposed to the elements: "the combination of cold and wet on an open bridge, with the wind blowing at you, and you can't blink an eye or you'd miss a signal, wasn't nice."[28]

Aboard *Oakville*, Russell explained what it was like for the ship to negotiate large waves:

> You'd sit right on top of a wave, maybe as big as 30 feet high, and you can hear the screw running but doing nothing as its sticking out of the water, the whole ship vibrating some-

thing terrible. Then, it would take a nose-dive off the wave and water would come up the fo'c'sle and slam into the bridge, filling up the gunwales up the side of the corvette![29]

Conditions inside the ship were far from comfortable. John Stevens, aboard the corvette HMCS *Galt*, said, "When you hit rough weather, it got so rough sometimes you couldn't stand up hardly … it was just like a cork floating on the water."[30] And a corvette's tendency to roll suddenly made it even more challenging for those within. Stewart recalls eating in the mess deck aboard HMCS *Stellarton* when the weather took a turn for the worse:

> I was sitting on a bench at the mess table, about eight guys to a table, with my back towards the lockers that lined the bulkhead when all of a sudden the ship rolled. No hints or anything that it was about to happen — corvettes could do that because of their round hulls you see. Well, I went flying and the guys hit the table so hard that they tore it out of the deck. It was bolted down of course, so you can imagine how hard they hit it. All eight of us, along with the table, went flying into the other table and guys next to us. Would you believe none of us got hurt?[31]

The north Atlantic was frequently a grey heaving mass of high rollers and biting winds, and when on deck sailors were instructed to hold onto the aptly named lifelines. As Russell explained: "if you didn't, when you hit one of those big waves, it would put you right overboard and that would be it."[32] It was not uncommon to be swept right off your feet by the waves. Stewart noted that at sea, "the real enemy was the weather in the north Atlantic, even in the summer it was bloody cold!"[33]

As in all corvettes, ratings would sleep in a hammock, which Russell said "was just as good as a bed."[34] He remembered sleeping over the mess deck table in the forward mess aboard *Oakville*, which was the seamans' mess deck. Every morning he would lash up his hammock and prepare the mess for breakfast. Stewart, on the other hand, would cramp-up in his hammock: "you'd sleep head to toe," he said, "the guy beside you slept opposite to you so someone's toes were always right in your face. At least the motion of the ship would put you to sleep while in a hammock."[35]

The food was one thing that Russell was quick to compliment: "One thing is that the food was good and there was always lots of it."[36]

Aboard *Galt*, Stevens similarly spoke highly of the cuisine. His ship had "... two good cooks and I don't remember having a bad meal."[37] Canadian corvettes were frequently on the "triangle run"

from New York, to Halifax, to St. John's, and were able to keep their galleys stocked with fresh rations. Sailors would eat porridge, scrambled eggs — sometimes even fried eggs — with toast for breakfast, and meat and potatoes for lunch and supper. It was "... all good food and hot," Russell said, "and there were snacks such as toast and jam and lots and lots of coffee."[38] However, the food aboard corvettes was only as good as the cook who prepared it. Alex Bramson, who was an able seaman in the Royal Canadian Naval Volunteer Reserve (RCNVR), had nothing but poor memories of the food aboard his corvette: "We had potatoes, one kind — boiled and the cook started cooking eggs at six in the morning and by the time we came in to eat them at eight, we called them rubber eggs."[39] Eating aboard a corvette, like all things, was challenging. As Stewart explained: "you had to hang onto whatever you were drinking or eating or it would go on you." A corvette typically only had one cook aboard ship, with a leading hand to assist, although a cook could usually count on defaulters* to send a hand into the galley to assist with cleaning or peeling potatoes. Sailors would eat before and after they came off their watch, "so the cook had a meal ready every four hours."[40]

When off duty, sailors aboard corvettes passed time by playing music (some ships even had pianos) and cards, or found a relatively quiet and dry spot to read a book. They would also have showers, which were taken with warm salt water. At noon, a sailor would receive a tot of rum**, usually just before, or directly after, their watch. Stewart was only sixteen and a half when he received his first ration of rum:

HMCS *Oakville*'s cook, P.J. McKeown, with his helper Richard Middleton from Toronto, October 1943. (*Courtesy P.J. McKeown.*)

* A sailor who committed an infraction aboard ship would be put on "defaulters," which became synonymous for being punished. David F. Stewart remembers what it was like: "This one time I got in trouble for sleeping-in and missing my duties. The quartermaster had came to wake me up for a special call, but I wasn't fully awake when he spoke to me and ended up going back to sleep. Well, then the Yeoman came and got me — he was a big, rough sort. Anyways, he comes down swearing at me and says 'That reflected directly on me — don't you ever do that again. Three days to defaulters!' He reported me to the captain, who gave me the punishment. I had to mop-up and clean the Chief's and PO's mess and their dishes. That was a tough job."

** Known as "Up Spirits," the last issue of Rum in the RCN was March 31, 1972, almost two years after the RN, who abolished the practice on July 31, 1970. A tot of rum was a sailor's daily ration, which equalled one-eighth of a pint during the Second World War.

You could take a tot of rum or take 10 cents a day. You couldn't save the rum and you got it neat, but you had to add coke or water in front of the officer to ensure you didn't save it — that was a problem. Some guys would save it and get drunk later, which they wanted to avoid.[41]

There was a great amount of "ribbing" that went around, especially between the trades. Stewart remembered: "Everyone referred to the signalmen as 'ladies,' while the gunners called communicators 'non-combatants.'"[42] He also noted that "signalmen were the greatest guys to start a buzz aboard a ship! One time we told the crew that we'd received a message saying we were going into refit in Charleston, South Carolina. So all the men went and buzzed their hair. Turns out we

were actually going to the North Atlantic!"[43]

Over time, the small crew of six officers and 79 junior and senior rates would become a family, and a notably young one.

Russell made good friends with "his boss" aboard *Oakville*, a Ben Carson from Port Arthur. Carson was a year or two older than Russell, who had just turned 18, and took care of him whenever they went ashore. Even though the age gap was minimal, aboard a corvette it made a big difference. Both Russell and Bramson noted that a person who was 20 years old was the "old man in the mess deck,"[44] at least as far as ratings went. Throughout it all close bonds were forged, the kinds strengthened by a mutual dependency for survival. After 60 years Russell still has fond memories of his shipmates aboard *Oakville*: "You know, working with your shipmates and being at sea taught me a lot of good. I learnt to live with a bunch

HMCS *Oakville*'s Communication Branch, 1942. *Back Row*: Tel Bill Roberts, Sig R. Bradley, Sig W. Bond, Tel C. Matheson, Sig Mike Cheyne. *Front Row*: Ldg/Sig G. Ballinger, Coder Albert Beer, Tel Don McKirdy, Ldg/Tel D. Corbett, Coder Jack Ward. (*Courtesy Albert Beer.*)

of other guys that were like family. We looked out for each other the way a big brother does for a little brother and it made being out there easier for me."[45]

Although corvettes were far from comfortable for the sailors that served in them, what they lacked in design was made up for by their toughness and versatility. They could be used for just about anything, from patrolling and anti-submarine warfare to rescue work and minesweeping. Corvettes could also turn better than anything else afloat and run faster than a U-boat. They became known as "cheap and nasty," after Churchill remarked that they were cheap for the British to build and nasty for the enemy. With corvettes, the RCN got "bang for the buck," and, despite their shortcomings, they were well suited for the rough weather of the turbulent and cold north Atlantic. It would forge the backbone of the RCN, shouldering the brunt of Trans-Atlantic convoy duties, and, as naval historian Marc Milner observes, it was "the ship that launched the Royal Canadian Navy onto the world stage."[46]

Corvettes, along with the other ships of the RCN, played a vital role in the "Battle of the Atlantic," which ran from September 1939 to May 1945. Coined by Churchill, it was the fight that pitted supply convoys, the lifeblood of the European Allied offensive, against the wolves of the *Kriegsmarine*. Protecting these "sheep" was primarily the responsibility of the growing RCN, earning it the nickname "sheep dog navy." The name was well earned. From the beginning of the war to 1943, the RCN protected half of the convoys escorted across the North Atlantic route between America to Britain (a.k.a. the North Atlantic Run), considered the most crucial of all supply routes. By mid-1944, Canada was protecting them all.

In May 1941, the RCN established the Newfoundland Escort Force (NEF), the first "foreign" operational responsibility undertaken by the RCN (prior to 1949, Newfoundland was not yet a part of Canada).[47] Corvettes were the heart of the NEF since they had the sea-keeping capability and range to stream across the Atlantic. By November, the British began to realize that the RCN's NEF was working twice as hard as British convoy groups. The Americans also took notice. Appalled by the Atlantic's turbulent weather and the brutally demanding escort cycle, they "… could only look on at the Canadians in wonder: at what they did under the impossible conditions, at their small ships surviving the vile weather (they ought to receive submariner's pay, one USN [United States Navy] Old Salt recalled, 'the corvettes spent so much time underwater!'), and at how anything enduring could be built under such dreadful conditions."[48] The RCN was growing a reputation for being tough — the faithful sheep dog protecting its flock from the German wolves waiting to intercept. Although the United States Navy (USN) assisted at first with Atlantic convoy duties, after the attack on Pearl Harbor on December 7, 1941, American naval focus shifted to the war in the Pacific. The Japanese attack had locked the RCN into the North Atlantic escort role. American forces slowly began to trickle out of the North Atlantic, and by early 1942, they left the RCN to carry on in the Western Atlantic while they focused on the war in the Pacific.

By the summer of 1944 the whole Trans-Atlantic convoy system was under Canadian escort, and nearly 40 percent of support groups (groups of elite submarine hunters) hunting U-boats in the Eastern Atlantic were RCN.[49] The British Admiralty even entertained the possibility of shifting its anti-submarine forces to the Pacific, leaving the Atlantic to the Canadians. By 1944 it was clear that the RCN was "… very good at what it did."[50] From humble origins, it would become the most feared anti-submarine force of any of the allies.

By war's end, the RCN multiplied by a factor of 50 to reach 100,000 men and women and over 400 fighting ships, with more than 900 vessels. After Britain and the United States, the RCN constituted the third largest navy in the world. It was the most dramatic leap of any nation's navy in history. During the course of the war, the RCN would be responsible for escorting 25,343 merchant ships carrying 181,643,180 tons of supplies across the North Atlantic. It would also be responsible for sinking 31 U-boats,[51] one of which was sunk by a corvette called *Oakville*.

HMCS *OAKVILLE*

The story of HMCS *Oakville* begins at a shipping yard in Port Arthur, Ontario. There, on February 1, 1941, the Port Arthur Shipbuilding Co. received the contract to build her and seven other corvettes. She was part of a larger order of 46 steel anti-submarine craft of the "whaler catcher" design, which had been split with two other Ontario-based shipyards in Collingwood and Kingston, as well as various other Quebec firms. These ships were to have a base value of $528,000 each, although contracts reported higher figures to accommodate the extra provisions necessary to make the vessels capable of navigating through the Great Lakes' canals. Newspapers listed the approximate value of the Ontario contracts as $10,000,000 and Quebec as $13,000,000, and upon completion the total value of the completed order was to be roughly $25,000,000. These "special" ships were described by newspapers as "submarine chasers," a new weapon to confront the growing threat of German U-boats. The 46 ships were to be divided between the RCN and RN.

Oakville's yard, originally the Western Dry Docks and Shipbuilding Company Ltd. of Port Arthur, entered a construction agreement with the city of Port Arthur in 1906, and in 1916 was purchased by the Port Arthur Shipbuilding Co. under capitalist James Whalen. The company was responsible for building a variety of vessels, ranging from tugs to passenger ships, and also operated as a dry dock facility for repairing and docking ships. During the First World War, it built ships for both the Canadian Merchant Marine and British Admiralty, including seagoing freighters, armed naval trawlers, and seagoing merchant ships. Following a period of stagnation from 1924–1940, where it relied heavily on repair work and manufacturing paper mill machinery, it once again started building ships for the Canadian Government and British Admiralty. With a modern and active machine and boiler shop, it could easily produce the engines, boilers, and hulls for corvettes, and even received contracts to produce a fleet of Algerine-class minesweepers.[52] *Oakville*'s keel was laid on December 21, 1940, and six months later she was launched on June 21, 1941.

H.M.C.S. OAKVILLE 1941
Corvette • Flower Class • Royal Canadian Navy • World War II

HMCS *Oakville* by artist Ian L. Morgan. Although the image indicates the year as 1941, the position of *Oakville*'s mast behind the bridge indicates that the drawing was made from an image of the ship after its fo'c'sle was extended, which was not completed until March 29, 1944. (*Courtesy Edward Stewart.*)

Arial shot of HMCS *Oakville*. Note the placement of the mast ahead of the bridge. (*Courtesy Edward Stewart.*)

With regards to her hull, *Oakville* was a typical short fo'c'sle corvette, although it would later be extended in 1944. She was 205 feet long, with a beam of 33 feet, a draught of 11.5 feet, and displaced 950 gross tons. The forward portion of the hull was devoted to accommodation — officer quarters, wardroom, and respective messes for seamen and stokers. Although sleeping conditions for the officers and petty officers were reasonable, the seamen were crowded in the stuffy and often wet forecastle. *Oakville*'s mid-ship was comprised entirely of two fire-tube boilers and an engine room. The machinery here was simple, cheap, and tough — easy for the marine engineer to operate and maintain. Her two Scotch marine boilers had a large reserve of steam, which could be harnessed for quick bursts of speed, ideal for intercepting and chasing surfaced submarines. However, their size limited the capacity of the fuel storage tanks, keeping her range to 3,500 miles at 12 knots, or 2,500 at a maximum speed of 16 knots. *Oakville*'s engine was similarly durable and uncomplicated — a single four-cycle triple-expansion

reciprocating steam engine that generated 2,750 horsepower. The rest of the ship aft of the engine room was devoted to another smaller mess, as well as the tiller flats and storage.

It was not large, even for the small crew. Enlisted members were exclusively reservists, with the exception of some regular force or recalled personnel who filled senior non-commissioned appointments, such as coxswain, chief boatswain's mate, gunlayer, and chief engineer. Officers were also taken from the reserves, with the exception of the captain, who could be ex-merchant navy.[53]*

With regards to armament, *Oakville* was equipped with a 4-inch (102-mm) Mk. IX breech-loading gun on her bow, usually situated on the fo'c'sle. Dating back to the First World War, it was designed as an anti-torpedo boat weapon for British battleships. It utilized 31-pound

---

* Marc Milner, in *Canada's Navy: The First Century*, (Toronto: University of Toronto Press, 1999), 91–92, notes that ships were commissioned faster than crews could be adequately trained. Officers were given speedy, rudimentary training, and if fortunate, were guided by a good RCNR (Royal Canadian Naval Reserve) captain, who would most likely be the only person onboard who could navigate.

shells, which it could fire a distance of 12,000 yards, though its accuracy was poor due to the corvette's lively nature. The weapon was better suited for intimidating U-boats, forcing them to submerge where the ship could make use of its other principal weapon — dreaded and powerful depth charges. HMCS *Oakville* had two depth-charge stern rails with a compliment of 40 depth charges, as well as four Mk. II depth-charge throwers on either side of the engine room casing.[54*]

Oakville Able Seaman George Kahan recounted the difficulties of securing depth charges aboard a corvette:

> On watch I dreaded to report depth charges loose, as the order would come back to go and secure them. Three hundred pounds of rolling garbage can — fight that and the rolling ship. Quite the feat. One time me and the VA had to do it. A big green one came over the side and dropped on us. We did not know where we were. I thought I was over the side and tried to swim. The wave threw me against the depth charge rack and just about put me out. The VA got a dislocated shoulder.[55]

Original British plans called for secondary armament of a two-pounder gun aft and 20-mm Oerlikons on the bridge. However, due to shortages, RCN corvettes were instead equipped with two twin .50 Browning machine guns as well as two twin .303 Lewis machine guns, which not only left the ship vulnerable to aircraft attack, but were also useless against the outer hull of a submarine.[56] Interestingly, written testimony from Executive Officer (XO) Lt. Cdr Kenneth B. Culley RCNVR indicates that *Oakville* was in fact fitted with "anti-aircraft mountings."[57] Additional sources support this claim, such as a newspaper picture of "anti-aircraft gunner" Ordinary Seaman Douglas Maclean onboard *Oakville*, manning what appears to be a 20-mm Oerlikon AA gun, as well as historical

works that mention the use of 20-mm guns during combat.[58] In addition to her guns, she was also fitted with hedgehogs (forward-throwing anti-submarine weapons). Kahan noted that they were "quite an apparatus. 24 bombs on spigots to be fired full speed ahead, then turn. Electric-impulse firing, lots of noise and we had to stand behind a plate for safety."[59]

Canadian corvettes also fell short of their British counterparts when it came to submarine detection equipment. While British corvettes were fitted with gyrocompasses and modern ASDICs, which made their depth-charge attacks notably more accurate, *Oakville* and her counterparts would have to make due with a magnetic compass and the antiquated 123A ASDIC.

Visibly, there were a few notable differences between Canadian and British corvettes. The RCN had originally conceived of corvettes as auxiliary minesweepers and had them constructed with a wider quarterdeck to accommodate handling the minesweeping equipment. Thus, the first 54 corvettes ordered by the RCN had broad, square sterns rather than the rounded "duck-tail" shape associated with corvettes of the RN. The structural change also meant that Canadian corvettes had their galley located to a more accessible position above the number one boiler room.[60]

In addition, Canadian corvettes also differed in their positioning of the after gun tub. While the British positioned theirs between the funnel and engine room skylight, the RCN moved it to aft of the engine room casing.

ANCHOR'S AWEIGH

During her construction, her Commanding Officer (CO), Lieutenant Alex C. Jones RCNR (Royal Canadian Naval Reserve), and XO Lieutenant Kenneth Culley RCNVR, were "ordered to stand by the ship under construction in Port Arthur."[61] During this time, Jones began receiving correspondence from the town of Oakville. The town was then a conservative riding and desired to show the Liber-

---

* Sources indicate that *Oakville* was equipped with four throwers, although two appears to have been the standard during construction.

al government how to properly run the war effort. The christening of a corvette provided the perfect opportunity. A member of the Oakville Corvette Committee, Frank Pullen, paid both the officers and the ship a visit in Port Arthur. Apparently their idea struck a cord with the ship's captain; after the meeting, Jones would visit the committee in Oakville several times to help make arrangements for the ship's christening, including securing the ceremony's guests of honour.

When the ship was finally finished, she was given a coat of paint. On her bow was written "K178" — her unique identification indicating both class and number. And so, on that warm summer's day in 1941, her hull still untouched by the ocean's salt, HMCS *Oakville* sailed out of Port Arthur and proceeded south down Lake Superior, the start of a long journey that would see her travel to many distant places. This submarine catcher had been well constructed and was ready to fulfil her role, but before that could happen she had two important functions to attend: her christening and commissioning. Her first order of business was thus in Lake Ontario, at the shores of her namesake town, where she would be officially made into a ship of war.

CHAPTER 2
A Glimmer of Hope

THE COMING ATTRACTION

The atmosphere in Canada during the early years of the Second World War was dark and solemn. For Canadians living during those troubled times, victory was anything but certain — an invasion of Britain seemed imminent, reports of U-boat attacks on convoys crossing the Atlantic filled headlines, and America had yet to fully commit to the war effort. There was little to raise the spirits of those worrying about loved ones or to silence fearful thoughts. A penetrating sombreness permeated each city and town, a feeling only exacerbated by daily casualty listings and incessant news updates. The war, both distant and close, inevitably plagued the minds of every citizen back home.

It is odd to think that a warship — something so connected to the very thing troubling Canadians — could inspire a sense of hope; yet for the town of Oakville, Ontario, a warship did just that. On November 5, 1941, residents celebrated, pushing aside their fears and kindling a resilient hope. The christening and adoption of HMCS *Oakville* by the community was a spectacle that not only attracted government

dignitaries, throngs of journalists, and crowds by the thousands, but brought a small town to national and international attention, if only for a short time. *Oakville* was embraced by her namesake town, its crew showered with gifts and warm memories to comfort them during the days ahead. In doing so, Oakville residents affirmed their commitment to the war.

From Pullen's visit to Port Arthur, it was clear that *Oakville*'s christening was eagerly anticipated. A great deal of excitement surrounded the coming attraction, and the committee in charge of the celebration spared little expense to commemorate the day. The event began making headlines as early as October 25, with the *Hamilton Spectator* announcing that "Oakville Plans Great Ceremony for Christening," noting further that "Government, and Naval Officials Will Participate in Dedication."[1] Assigning a full column to the article, the *Spectator* excited readers, indicating that the corvette committee was in the process of finalizing the event and that the date for the christening would be set as Wednesday, November 5.[2] It promised citizens of Oakville that the day would be "important in the town's history" and listed the names of 11 local students (although a twelfth would later be added) who had been voted by their peers to represent each school in the district and present gifts to the ship's crew.[3] On the day of the ceremony, these fortunate few would travel to Toronto to board the ship and accompany its commander, Lieutenant A.C. Jones,[4] and his crew of 60 men for the hour journey to the town of Oakville.

Joining these children was none other than the Hon. Angus L. Macdonald, Minister of National Defence for Naval Affairs, and Rear-Admiral Percy W. Nelles, Chief of Naval Staff (CNS).

Rear-Admiral Percy W. Nelles (left) and the Hon. Angus L. Macdonald in Toronto, prior to boarding HMCS *Oakville* for its christening. (*Courtesy Edward Stewart.*)

Accompanying them were representatives of neighbouring municipalities, and presidents of 36 organizations "engaged in war work."[5] As for the ceremony in Oakville, the *Spectator* mentioned that a "massed choir in robes" would participate in welcoming the ship, and that a special evening banquet at the Oakville Club would be held, "to which 300 will be invited, and for which an excellent program is being prepared."[6] Lastly, the article noted that the citizens of Oakville planned to adopt the ship and provide its crew with some comforts, with specific mention of a library.

The "adopting" of *Oakville* by the community is a significant aspect of christening a ship off the shores of its hometown. It serves a threefold purpose: to provide the crew with a specific community to defend so as to elevate their sense of purpose and morale, to give the folks at home a sense of contributing in concrete ways to the war effort, and to enable citizens to identify with the RCN's mission. *Oakville*'s christen-

ing forged a common sense of purpose and a reciprocal relationship between the community and its crew. *Oakville* would valiantly defend its hometown, and, in turn, the hometown supported its champion.

A day before the parade's scheduled date, the *Toronto Evening Telegram* announced "Oakville Agog as Day Nears for Ceremony."[7] Alluding to the town's history as a once thriving port, the *Telegram* wrote that the town would "re-live some of the faded glory of a thriving shipbuilding center" with the arrival of the newly built corvette for its christening. It had once been the birthplace of some of the "staunchest 'hearts of oak' that ever dipped their bows into the waves of the Great Lakes."[8] Describing the "enthusiasm" of Oakville residents, the reporter notes that this "all-important" ceremony would "start the vessel on a career more grim than that of the white-winged boats which peacefully nosed their way into lake harbors to pick up assorted cargo"[9] — *Oakville*, unlike the merchant ships that sailed from the town's port, was a ship of war.

At this time, it was common for dredges, tugs, and freighters to pass along Oakville's shores, uploading coal and other resources. Situated at the centre of a population of 1,500,000 within a 50-mile radius, Oakville's shore-based location midway between Toronto and Hamilton made it ideal for manufacturing (a decade later, in 1951, the Oakville Ford plant would be created). Regionally, it was, as it remains presently, one of the highest population densities in the country, giving the town a strong market potential and a diversified, skilled workforce. Oakville was, as the ceremony programme boasted, "an address of which to be proud."

More information about the preliminary event was provided, detailing that committee member J.R. Rodger and chairman Dr. M.E. Lunau would take the school children to Toronto to board the corvette. Estimated time for the ship's arrival in Oakville was 2:00 p.m. at Lakeside Park.[10] A request from the committee also appears in the article, asking that all members of church choirs in town be assembled by 1:45 p.m. "in the specially constructed stand to lead the hymn singing during the christening ceremony."[11] Even "former members" were urged to participate, and the town band would be in attendance. An impressive reception was in the works. A separate banquet in the gymnasium of St. John's United Church was to be provided for the participating Sea Cadets,[12] and an informal dance at Victoria Hall was to conclude the event, with all proceeds to be used to purchase further comforts for *Oakville*'s crew. The event was also to be broadcast by CHML Hamilton with Norman Marshall as the announcer. The ceremony promised to be a splendid event for all.

NELLES AND MACDONALD

The christening ceremony of HMCS *Oakville* had two important dignitaries in attendance, both notable figures in Canadian history. The appearance of both the CNS and Minister of Defence for Naval Services at this celebration helps to mark the significance of the day. As important figures in Canada's war effort, they understandably garnered much press; in a time of war and uncertain victory, the nation hung on the words uttered from these men's lips. Although their speeches and actions on November 5 were very much geared towards the town of Oakville and its namesake ship, they were equally directed to all Canadians.

Percy Walker Nelles can be confidently labelled a Canadian naval legend. The first Canadian to be appointed CNS in 1934, he is frequently credited with keeping the Canadian navy alive during the Depression. A native of Brantford, Ontario, he was born on January 7, 1892. His father was an officer in the Royal Canadian Dragoons, and, although Nelles was focused on a military career at a young age, he intended to venture on his own path rather than follow directly in his father's footsteps. In 1908, at age 16, his application for cadet placement in the Canadian Naval Service was accepted and he was posted aboard a Canadian Fisheries schooner — the second of only two candidates accepted (although the other student would withdraw).* Two years later, he was appointed a midshipman-in-training aboard HMCS *Niobe*, one of

* The other candidate, F.A. Campbell, had been accepted first by Kingsmill, the first director of the Canadian Naval Service. When Campbell withdrew, Nelles was the only member of the class of 1908.

the first two ships in the newly formed RCN, in which Nelles was the founding recruit. In 1911, he was sent overseas to Britain to complete his naval training and was selected, along with 37 other cadets, to represent the Canadian navy at the coronation ceremony of King George V. He continued his training aboard HMS *Dreadnought* and in 1914 became consecutively a sub-lieutenant and lieutenant aboard HMS *Suffolk*, where he notably "participated in protecting British interests at Vera Cruz during the Mexican Revolution."[13] He lastly served aboard HMS *Antrim* in 1916 before accepting a staff officer position in 1917.

Nelles worked as the flag lieutenant to the Director of the Canadian Naval Service at Naval Service Headquarters in Ottawa until 1922, attaining the rank of lieutenant-commander and completing an RN intelligence course. He then alternated between shore and sea assignments with both the RN and RCN, attending both the RN's College Staff Course (1925) and Senior Officer's Technical Course (1929). During this time he was promoted to the rank of commander and was made the CO Pacific Coast. In 1930, he assumed the responsibilities of XO of the Bermuda-based light-cruiser HMS *Dragon*, where he soon became acting-captain after his CO passed away. This was the first time a Canadian had been given such a command. Following this, he was made the CO of the new Canadian River-class destroyer, HMCS *Saguenay*, the first warship built specifically for the Canadian fleet. In addition, he was also made the senior officer of the Canadian destroyer flotilla. After a year at sea, he was made commander-in-charge of HMCS *Stadacona* in 1932.

Nelles's progression through the navy continued. A year later, he was made a full naval captain and attended the Imperial Defence College. He then received the position of CNS and rank of commodore. It was a post he would hold for an entire decade, and during his tenure he would rise through the ranks to become a vice-admiral in 1941. During this period, he was not only responsible for seeing the navy through the economic problems of the 1930s, but also guided the massive wartime expansion of the RCN. He acted as the Canadian Technical Advisor at the London Naval Conference in 1935–1936, and, with constant pressure from both local and Allied governments, he enabled Canada to become a major player in the Battle of the Atlantic.[14]

In 1944, following a bitter disagreement with Angus L. Macdonald over naval expansion, he was sent to London as the Senior Canadian Flag Officer Overseas, where he was put in charge of coordinating RCN operations for D-Day. During the invasion, he was actually aboard a RCN destroyer and motor torpedo boat to observe the proceedings. As author Arthur Bishop, himself a Second World War veteran, simply explained: "Nelles was in the thick of the naval action."[15] He retired from the navy on January 6, 1945, and was promoted a day later to full admiral (retired), the highest rank a naval officer can achieve.

During his career, Nelles received several noteworthy accolades, including Companion — Order of the Bath, Commander — Legion of Merit (USA); Commander — Legion of Honour (France); Croix de Guerre with Palme en Bronze (France); and Knight First Class — Order of St. Olav (Norway). He died shortly after the war on June 13, 1951 and was buried at sea from HMCS *Sault Ste. Marie* with full honours. A Royal Canadian Sea Cadet Corps (formed in 1941) is named after him in his hometown, as well as a barracks at Canadian Forces Base (CFB) Esquimalt.

Angus Lewis Macdonald, popularly known as "Angus L.," is by reputation the most important and influential politician in Nova Scotia's modern history.[16] Born on August 10, 1890 at Dunvegan, Inverness County, on Cape Breton Island, he was educated at both Port Hood Academy and St. Francis Xavier University. While earning his degree, the drums of war sounded, and in 1915 he started military training in the Canadian Officers Training Corps. In February of the following year, he joined the ranks of the 185th battalion — the Cape Breton Highlanders — and left for Britain in October. He continued training, was promoted to the rank of lieutenant, and in the waning years of the war was finally sent to the trenches of France to serve with Nova Scotia's 25th battalion. There, Macdonald saw fierce combat. During one engagement he even had cause to lead his entire company because all the senior officers had been killed or seriously wounded.[17] He suffered his own wounds during the war, taking a German sniper's bullet in the neck a mere four days before the Armistice was signed. He spent eight months in a British hospital before finally being able to return home, having done his part for "king and country."

After the First World War, Macdonald returned to education, attending Dalhousie Law School for two years and earning a law degree in 1921. Upon graduating, he accepted a job as assistant deputy attorney general with the government of Nova Scotia, and in 1924 became a full-time university lecturer. After attaining his doctoral degree from Harvard Law School, he resigned from his lecturing position to seek a new career in politics. After a failed attempt to obtain the federal riding of Inverness, he moved with his family to Halifax where he opened a law practice.

Focused on his political ambitions, Macdonald began working with the provincial Liberal party, and in the convention of 1930 he was unexpectedly nominated and voted in as the new party leader. After his victory, he began touring the province where his gifts as a political orator quickly became apparent. Fighting against the governing Conservative party, Macdonald soon developed a reputation as a crusader for the common person's rights, a modern-day Joseph Howe fighting to re-instil responsible government in Nova Scotia.[18] His party easily won the 1933 election.

During his first term as premier, Macdonald led the province out of the Depression through a wave of public work, pension, and social relief programs. He also successfully boosted Nova Scotia's appeal as a popular travel destination, attracting lucrative tourism by promoting a romanticized highland Scottish culture.[19] In March of 1937, Macdonald's Liberals actually recorded a surplus, the first time the province had done so in 14 years. During that year's election, his party won an even greater majority in the provincial legislature.[20]

The Second World War brought a sudden change to Macdonald's political career. He again found himself heeding the call to arms, although this time it would not be as a soldier. Mackenzie King, under pressure to recruit the best Canadians to fill his wartime cabinet, personally requested that Macdonald take the post of minister of national defence for naval services. In 1940, Macdonald left provincial politics and was sworn into the federal cabinet. He spent the next five years in the federal government, and, working alongside Nelles, took on the gargantuan task of building Canada's naval forces. During this time, he also played a significant role in the conscription crisis. Although Mackenzie King, due to election promises, did not favour imposing mandatory military service, Macdonald felt it necessary should voluntary recruitment fail. A former frontline solider, he felt strongly about this issue, and did not think it fair that able-bodied Canadians avoided their patriotic duty while others made the supreme sacrifice.

By the end of the war, Macdonald had grown to dislike federal politics and resigned. He returned to the leadership of the provincial Liberal party and regained the premiership in 1945. With the rallying call, "All's Well With Angus L.,"[21] Macdonald and his Liberals seemed unbeatable. He had endeared himself to his constituents, becoming, as author Ian McKay explains, "a man of the people — not 'Mr. Macdonald,' but 'Angus L.'"[22] Macdonald remained primer to the last, dying in office in 1954.

An estimated 100,000 people attended Macdonald's funeral in Halifax. The Halifax *Mail Star* wrote that he was the "most beloved Nova Scotia statesman and scholar since Joseph Howe."[23] Macdonald's "long career as a provincial politician … made him the most revered premier in the history of Nova Scotia."[24] He has been memorialized in several ways, most notably by the "Angus L. Macdonald" bridge, connecting Halifax to Dartmouth (1955), and a library named in his honour at St. Francis Xavier University (1965).

A DAY TO REMEMBER

The christening on November 5, 1941 drew the largest crowds the town of Oakville has arguably ever seen.[25] The *Toronto Daily Star* exclaimed "Thousands Pack Shoreline for Oakville's Christening," while the *Telegram* wrote "Christen Corvette 'Oakville' As Entire Town Watches." In fact, over 2,000 people were reported to be on the scene, including locals from neighbouring communities and a slew of reporters. Pictures of the event corroborate these reports — people were looking forward to a spectacular event, and were eager to steal their first glimpse of the corvette as it approached from the east.

Papers had also been anticipating this event and gave full-page coverage, complete with pictures of the ceremony and ship. It even appeared on the front page of the *New York Times* and cropped up in the *London Times*. Admittedly, coverage in non-Canadian media focused primarily on the speeches that were made by Macdonald and Nelles; however, that the town of Oakville even made it into these papers signifies the importance of this occasion.

Philip Shaw was 15 years old when his father took him from their home in Port Credit, Mississauga to see the event. Although it was a typical dull November day, there was excitement in the air and Shaw knew that he was going to witness what he called an "historic event."[26]

Before her arrival in Oakville, 12 school children were picked up early in the day and shuttled to Toronto. With all the anticipation surrounding the event, they must have been in high spirits, and the presence of Macdonald and Nelles certainly must have added to their excitement. The CNS was first to board her with Macdonald on his heels.

Nelles and Macdonald en-route to board HMCS *Oakville*. Note: this occurred in Oakville, after the ship had departed Toronto. (*Courtesy Edward Stewart.*)

Nelles pauses for some pictures while boarding HMCS *Oakville*. (*Courtesy Edward Stewart.*)

School children pose with senior rates aboard HMCS *Oakville*. (*Courtesy Edward Stewart.*)

Nelles and Macdonald pose with local school children chosen to travel aboard HMCS *Oakville* from Toronto to its namesake town. (*Courtesy Edward Stewart.*)

Gene Delaney, who would present the crew with a silk ensign, poses in a hammock with crewmembers of HMCS *Oakville*. (*Courtesy Edward Stewart*.)

Image of crowds gathered at Lakeside Park in Oakville, November 5, 1941. Note: HMCS *Oakville* has already arrived and is anchored in the distance. (*Courtesy Edward Stewart*.)

Boatswains aboard *Oakville* piped the side while Lieutenant A.C. Jones, waiting at the edge of the gangplank, paid compliments to the rear admiral. Once all parties were aboard, the ship prepared to depart and by 1:00 it had slipped from the Toronto jetty. During the trip, school children mingled with the crew, explored the ship, spoke with the cabinet minister and CNS, and posed for several pictures.

Oakville's trim grey hull was sighted on the lake as it approached the town around noon. As planned, the ship's anchor was dropped at 2:00 p.m., though it stayed offshore due to the shallow depths of water near Lakeside Park, which prevented her from properly berthing at the nearby pier. However, she was in plain sight for everyone to see, and, unable to contain their enthusiasm, the shoulder-to-shoulder crowd along the shore erupted into cheers — *Oakville* had finally arrived.

A small launch boat, *Esperanza*, ferried Macdonald, Nelles, and the 12 students ashore. They were greeted by what the *Toronto Daily Star* called a "picturesque setting"[27] — school children, boy scouts, sea cadets, district heads, Oakville and Trafalgar civil guards, girl guides, representatives of all community and civic organizations, and a unit of the Royal Australian Air Force. Beyond this,

the entire town appeared "combined to a man to do honour to the occasion … gathered around the raised platform at the waterfront park."[28] It was as warm a greeting as could ever be received.

Mayor Murray F. "Doc" Deans, a dentist by trade, welcomed the dignitaries, who then followed Nelles and Macdonald as they inspected the guard of honour. This included members of the Toronto and Hamilton RCNVR, sea cadets, and notably the squad of Australian Airmen.[29]

After the inspection, the procession headed to the platform, where Frank Pullen, a local man with strong family connections to the RCN and who held the rank of major, introduced Nelles to the crowd. Pullen's connection to the RN went back generations, and two of his sons were already serving in the RCN — Lieutenant-Commander Hugh Francis Pullen (later to become Rear-Admiral Pullen OBE, CD, RCN) had just over a month ago received command of a newly acquired destroyer from the United States Navy, *St. Francis*, while Lieutenant Thomas Charles Pullen was currently serving aboard Canada's senior ship, *Assiniboine*. In addition, his third son, Captain Ernest G. Pullen, worked at army headquarters in Ottawa, while his daughter, Nanette, served as an

Esperanza bringing dignitaries and guests ashore. (*Courtesy Edward Stewart.*)

Nelles inspects a Royal Australian Air Force unit at Lakeside Park in Oakville (*Courtesy Edward Stewart.*)

ambulance driver in the Royal Army Medical Corps. She was in France before its capitulation and was currently stationed in England. Theirs was an Oakville family firmly committed to duty and country.

Nelles spoke openly to the crowd, commenting that: "HMCS *Oakville* could not have been christened at a more appropriate time"[30] and, explaining the importance of corvettes for the RCN, pointed out that "it is to Oakville's undying honour that a Corvette shall carry her name into the Empire's battle-line."[31] He continued: "Corvettes like HMCS *Oakville* are proving their worth in the Battle of the Atlantic, which we're darn well going to win."[32] The crowd roared in support.

As a principal architect of the RCN's rapid mobilization, Nelles stressed that "it was from a very small nucleus that we were able to build a sizeable navy," though he urged that "we must have more ships and we must have more men." The CNS explained in further detail:

Since the start of hostilities we have increased our forces by an almost incredible amount and today our craft afloat number close to 300, with personnel being about 27,000 men. Both ships and men are daily increasing. But, I don't want you to mistaken me. We have not yet got sufficient ships or sufficient men for the task as we see it.[33]

Nelles's message that day was two-pronged: although he was there to give the crowd hope by stating his confidence in their namesake corvette, he also was keen to motivate people to take a more active role in the war movement. Considering his station, his words must have carried significant weight with the assembly.

Following Nelles's speech was the christening ceremony. Again, the officials boarded *Esperanza* to travel to the ship, all the while accompanied by the choir ashore singing "Rule Britannia." They came alongside *Oakville*'s port-side hull, just behind the bow anchor's chain, which faced Lakeside Park, and were greeted by siren blasts from the corvette and whistles from ashore.[34] Reverend Canon D. Russell Smith, rector of St. Jude's Anglican Church, officiated over the religious proceedings and dedicated the vessel:

> In the Faith of Jesus Christ, on behalf of His Gracious Majesty King George VI, and in the name of the Father, the Son, and the Holy Ghost we Christen His Majesty's Canadian Corvette 'Oakville.'[35]

Following this, the naval prayer was recited, as well as a special blessing for the gifts that would be given to the ship by the community. The mayor's wife, Mrs. P.M. Deans, then approached for the actual christening. Grasping a bottle of champagne dangling from a line attached to the ship's rail, she broke it against the freshly painted hull and proclaimed: "Godspeed and fair sailing to all those who serve in her."[36]

The golden liquid ran down the hull and met with the waters of Lake Ontario as *Oakville*'s CO, Lieutenant Jones, along with members of his crew, boarded the launch. They then proceeded back ashore to the distant singing of "There'll Always Be An England" — very poignant considering Germany's attacks on Britain, and certainly deeply felt by the corvette's crew, every one of them sworn into his majesty's service. The *Toronto Daily Star* interjects that around this time a formation of airplanes dove in salute for the newly christened warship, although it fails to mention if this occurred before or after the christening.[37]

Mrs. Deans prepares to christen HMCS *Oakville*. (*Courtesy Edward Stewart.*)

Launch coming alongside HMCS *Oakville* to pick up Jones and Culley. (*Courtesy Edward Stewart.*)

Dr. M.E. Lunau, Chair of the Oakville Corvette Committee, greets Jones ashore. (*Courtesy Edward Stewart.*)

Jones waves to the crowd while being escorted to the podium, Culley close behind. (*Courtesy Edward Stewart.*)

Dignitaries raising their hats and cheering the officers and crew of HMCS *Oakville*. (*Courtesy Edward Stewart.*)

Oakville's first commanding officer, Lieutenant A. C. Jones RCNR, addressing the crowd. (*Courtesy Edward Stewart.*)

Back on land, Jones and his entourage received a chorus of cheers from the assembled crowd. Members of the Oakville Corvette Committee then escorted the CO to the podium, where Nelles, Macdonald, Deans, and various other officials waited. Along the way, Jones smiled and waved to the masses, undoubtedly overwhelmed by the sheer numbers in attendance.

Once at the podium, he received a warm greeting by Mayor Deans, who welcomed him and his crew on behalf of the citizens. Announcing that this day was "one to be remembered,"[38] he elaborated the significance of the event for the community. He then proceeded, to the delight of the crowd, to officially adopt the officers and crew as honorary citizens of the town of Oakville.

It then came time for the first presentation of gifts by 11 of the 12 chosen school children. On behalf of his crew, Jones received the gifts, which were, in order:

- **Ship's Bell** — Murray Leonard of Oakville Central School
- **Ship's Clock** — Bill Adamson of Oakville High School
- **Radio (officer's mess)** — James Devonish of Oakville Separate School
- **Radio (petty officer's mess)** — Jack Cruickshank of Pine Grove School
- **Radio (crew quarters)** — Billie Louth of Pine View School
- **Radio (stoker quarters)** — Donald Munroe of Oakville Westwood School
- **Books for a Ship's Library (300 total)** — Vera Wilson of Maple Grove School
- **Knee-length Seaman's Windbreakers** — Jock Gairdner of Appleby College
- **Electric Percolators** — Wendy Auld of Linbrook School
- **Electric Plates** — Jock Chisholm of Oakville Brantwood School
- **Ditty Bags** (containing comforts knitted by the women of Oakville/district) — Lois Rodgers of Miss Lightbourne's School.[39]

Oakville resident Mrs. Marlatt displays HMCS *Oakville*'s bell and chronometer. (*Courtesy Edward Stewart.*)

In addition, the chairman of the Corvette Committee gave an unscheduled gift: a portrait of the King. After Jones accepted the portrait, Hughes Cleaver, Member of Parliament for Halton County and part of the Corvette Committee, stepped to the microphone to introduce the Minister of the Naval Service to the crowd.

In one of the spectacle's most interesting moments, Macdonald decided to disclose some important information to the assembled crowd and press. Checking quickly as to its advisability with Nelles, who replied simply "well, the Germans certainly know where they are and I'm going to say it publicly myself,"[40] Macdonald turned and announced that two U-boats had been attacked, and one possibly sunk, off the northern tip of Newfoundland during the previous month:

> Of the submarines we located at the Belle Isle channel, one was attacked by a Canadian corvette and possibly sunk and one was attacked by a Canadian costal patrol plane. There are many submarines now between Belle Isle and Iceland, and there are others along the southern convoy route [...] You can say there are submarines right off the coast of Newfoundland — that they are actually within sight of the shore. Naturally we are attacking them wherever we find them.[41]

The Minister of the Naval Service even went so far as to explain the cooperation between the navy and patrol planes of the Air Force Costal Command: "We usually find them by sound and attack them by depth charge. The airmen attack by bomb. We are working very closely together."[42] Turning his attention back to the ship, Macdonald applauded the citizens' efforts and commented that it was a real encouragement for a ship's company to be "adopted" by a town:

> It encourages the men of the navy when they realize that the people back home are behind them and are trying to make things as pleasant and

Jones responding to gifts presented to HMCS *Oakville*. (*Courtesy Edward Stewart.*)

as comfortable as possible for them. Believe me, these gifts are appreciated not only by the officers and ratings of HMCS *Oakville*, but by every member of the Canadian Navy.[43]

Macdonald then focused on the physical ship and stressed that *Oakville* had been built in a Lake Superior port "in the heart of the dominion, 1,000 miles from salt water."[44] The *Globe*'s journalist drew upon this point — Macdonald was showing that this corvette was through and through a Canadian ship. Canadian-built with a Canadian crew, it was truly a representation of the country — one of Canada's finest.

His words spoken, Macdonald stepped back from the microphone, whereupon the twelfth and final gift scheduled for the event was presented by Gene Delaney of Oakville High School. She offered to Lieutenant Jones a very symbolic present — a silk White Ensign for the ship. It would fly from *Oakville*'s stub mast, positioned between the funnel and the stern, marking her ascension to a full-fledge ship of His Majesty's Navy. All she required was her commission to set her off into the Atlantic.

Responding to the gifts, *Oakville*'s commander concluded with a heartfelt "thanks and thanks again."[45] Following the presentation, the officers and crew proceeded back to their ship, while the choir and band led the crowd in a sombre "For Those in Peril on The Sea," perhaps in symbolic recognition that *Oakville* would soon be in harm's way. Certainly, the papers made no mistake in this. The *Globe and Mail*'s title "HMCS Oakville Ready as Nazi Submarines Lurk Near" shows clearly what people expected of her, especially in light of the Minister of the Naval Service's disclosure.

Once aboard the ship, the crew held a small ceremony, raising the newly acquired Ensign as the choir ashore led all in "God Save the King." With the flag aloft for all to see, the ship commenced practice drills 1,000 feet offshore to show the crowd some of the corvette's capabilities. With her quick turning ability, *Oakville*'s nautical manoeuvres would have impressed the audience lining the shore.

The last event of the afternoon was a march past, with the salute taken by Macdonald from a stand erected in front of the post office on Colborne Street (present-day Lakeshore Road). Papers listed that the procession included the Australian Airmen, an RCNVR detachment from Toronto and Hamilton, members

Veterans of the First World War, marching in honour of HMCS *Oakville*'s christening. (*Courtesy Edward Stewart.*)

Members of either HMCS *York* or *Star* marching in the parade. (*Courtesy Edward Stewart.*)

of the Lorne Scots regiment, Oakville and Trafalgar Civil Guard, Canadian Legionnaires, Sea Cadets, school children, Boy Scouts, Cubs, and Girl Guides. Music for the march was supplied by Oakville's Citizens Band and the Lorne Scots Pipes and Drums. From the pictures that have survived, it is also clear that a bren gun carrier, as well as an army regiment other than the Lorne Scots were also present. The images of marching men, children, musicians, and the throng of spectators lining the street, declare the importance of this event. Never has there been another spectacle of such grandeur and significance in the town of Oakville.[46]

The banquet at the Oakville Club, which followed shortly after the parade at 6:30 p.m., was a more exclusive event, with only the more notable citizens of the community in attendance. The head table seated guests of honour Macdonald, Nelles, Jones, and his mother, Edith, as well as Mayor F. M. Deans, Reverend C.D. Smith, Mr. H. Cleaver, Mr. T.A. Blakelock, and Major F. Pullen, along with their respective spouses. Lieutenant-Commander E. Finch-Noyes RCNVR also occupied a seat at the head table. Seated before the head table were the 60 crewmembers of HMCS *Oakville*, members of the Australian Air Force, and several guests from out of town.

In naval fashion, dinner was served first, followed by a toast to the King. Mayor Deans then stood from his seat at the head table and addressed the guests, declaring that it had been a memorable day in the history of the town and that everyone in the district would be awaiting word of the exploits of the adopted crew and ship. He then presented a large silver wardroom tray to Lieutenant Jones, who in turn thanked the promoters on behalf of his mother and crew. His shipmates replied enthusiastically with "three lusty cheers for Oakville." Major Pullen then proposed, as per naval mess custom, a toast to His Majesty's Navy, while T.A. Blakelock, MPP, gave a toast to the mothers and wives of those at sea. Appropriately, Jones's mother was honoured with the presentation of a large bouquet of flowers and in reply declared: "I am only sorry that I did not have more sons to give to the navy, but I am going to make up for that by adopting the

HMCS *Oakville*."[47] Dr. Lunau of the corvette committee thanked the guests from Ottawa for being present and expressed the pleasure the citizens of the district felt in having the crew of *Oakville* as guests in their town. Cleaver ended the formalities by proposing a toast to the country: "Canada is a country united as never before."[48]

Macdonald, the famous orator, then delivered a powerful speech to the assembled guests and press:

> To-day there is only one grim thought of war. There was no choice for Canada when war came. This is nothing more or less than a struggle for domination by Hitler, who has set out to subjugate the world. We cannot fight a war with words. Munich brought not peace, but war. There is only one way to fight this war — build ships and planes and train men to know how to fight. Our country slept while Germany worked. A dreamer and pacifist has laid a spell on us. Now we have to make up for lost time. It's a race against time and a swift moving hell. Hitler's time-table just now is a little bit out of joint. Russia has earned the admiration of the world. England still remains unconquered and never will be enslaved by the hordes of Hitler. We are witnessing a total war with every one standing in the battle line. It is for us to be courageous and steadfast.[49]

Papers reported that the town continued in its celebrations until midnight, and the *Toronto Daily Star* concluded, quoting speakers of the committee during the banquet, "The Oakville district demonstrated the loyalty that has put 20 percent of its population in uniform."[50]

COMMISSIONED

The day after her christening, *Oakville* continued its journey, making a short stop in Burlington, Ontario, before heading east up the St. Lawrence. With comforting gifts and lingering memories to keep them company as they passed by various towns and cities along the way, the crew was provided a hint of the grandeur and splendour of the vast country for which they would be fighting. On November 18, the corvette reached Montreal, where she received her formal commission, though the event was unofficial in form, especially in comparison to her christening. As Culley himself explains, "there was a war on and we had to escort a couple of newly constructed Fairmile motor launches to Halifax — without delay."[51] Among those in attendance was none other than Lady Mountbatten, wife of the King's cousin, Lord Louis Mountbatten. It seemed that *Oakville* had a penchant for drawing out notable figures and attracting press. Among a class of small and unspectacular ships, she stood out.

Lady Mountbatten aboard HMCS *Oakville*. (*Courtesy Edward Stewart.*)

A CHAMPION SETS FORTH

After her commission, *Oakville* headed for Halifax to be fitted and conduct sea trials in preparation for her important role as a convoy escort. The ship actually "… sailed to Halifax without guns because of an old naval treaty with the United States that stipulated that no armed ships were allowed on the Great Lakes."[52] It was still a month before Pearl Harbor and America's entrance into the war.

December 1941 was anything but pleasant at sea aboard *Oakville*. Telegraphist W.J. Roberts recalled:

> Our first trip out was one of the worst and even up in the wireless cabin we were getting water on the deck, from where I don't know unless some of the rivets were leaking. We were escorting a very slow convoy about 3 to 4 knots so had to make a lot of broadside runs into the trough of the waves. I don't think it was all that necessary, but I know some of the crew were upset at a certain first lieutenant who spent his time kneeling to watch the roll indicator glass to see how far it would go.[53]

Shipmate Charlie Matthewson noted:

> We ran into the worst storm that I can ever remember. The waves were like mountains, smashing over the foredeck and into the wheelhouse. This seemed to last about 24 hours and when daybreak came the convoy was not to be seen. The Captain, Lieutenant [A.C.] Jones, examined the damage and decided to return to Halifax. It was enough to make repairs.[54]

On January 8, 1942, the crew bundled up against a cold North Atlantic Sea as the ship set off on her maiden voyage as part of the Western Local Escort

Ice accumulated aboard HMCS *Oakville*, taken in the North Atlantic during convoy duty. (*Courtesy P.J. McKeown.*)

Force (WLEF). It was a sharp contrast to the celebrations and warm cheer they had enjoyed in November, and the tossing and churning of the icy Atlantic, as well as the effects of *Oakville*'s wet and lively nature, most likely did nothing to soften the mental and physical blow to the crew. It was undoubtedly a sobering experience — a rude awakening to the task they had been trained to perform.

And their task was dangerous. The press surrounding the ship hinted at nothing less; with article headings such as "HMCS Oakville Ready as Nazi Submarines Lurk Near," little was left to the imagination. The public expected *Oakville* to fight. During the early years of the war, people in Allied nations felt the prospect of defeat deeply in their hearts, fuelling cheers at Nelles's proclamation that the RCN would "win" the Battle of the Atlantic with ships like HMCS *Oakville*. The citizens in attendance at *Oakville*'s christening ceremony looked to the ship and its crew with a sense of hope — they wanted *Oakville* to be up to the task, "ready" to fight for their country's sovereignty, and, more than that, be victorious. With articles posting headlines such as "German Submarine Menace Nearing Shore of Canada," they needed a champion.

Oakville provided them with a glimmer of hope to hold onto. The mayor's admission that "everyone in the district would be awaiting word of *Oakville*'s exploits," made clear that the townspeople had placed their hopes and faith in this ship and crew — *their ship*. They had chosen their champion.

As HMCS *Oakville* left harbour, with the turbulent North Atlantic before her, one wonders what the men must have felt about what lay before them. Did Jones or his crew find themselves drawn to the gifts that had been given to them by their namesake town? Did they remember the enjoyment or pride they felt that day in Oakville? Did they begin wondering about loved ones and the places they called home? And did Deans's words echo in their minds as they took in the vastness of the Atlantic before them? Could any of them have even guessed or felt that this tough, doughty corvette and its crew would grant those citizens what their hearts so keenly desired and live up to the hype that followed her every move?

Sailors aboard HMCS *Oakville* pose for a photo. (*Courtesy Edward Stewart.*)

CHAPTER 3
Dogs and Wolves

THE JOURNEY SOUTH

As part of the WLEF, *Oakville* was thrust into her designated escort role. Between January and June 1942, she took on a slew of convoy duties on routes between Newfoundland and New York, weathering the winter Atlantic through to the summer. During this time, she visited ports in Boston, New York, Saint John, and Sydney, and shore leave opportunities saw the crew immersing themselves in the local sights and sounds. Images still exist of crewmembers posing in New York bars and clubs, such as Keith Waddell's souvenir photo from the Metropole Hotel.

Jack Drysdale, an ASDIC operator in *Oakville* between 1942–1943, noted "New York was a great town for a serviceman. Subway fare was a nickel. Pepsi-Cola and a hotdog were 15 cents. Tickets were obtained from the USO [United Service Organization] for stage shows, pictures shows, lunches and suppers. So, you could have a dollar in your pants and have a real ball."[1] *Oakville* became a recurring sight for New Yorkers whose city was a familiar stop for the corvette's crew, an association that would later resurface.

After Japan's strike at the American Pacific fleet stationed at Pearl Harbor, U-boat attacks on Allied shipping in the western Atlantic took a dramatic turn. Hitler's wolfpack ruthlessly pursued merchant ships in U.S. coastal waters and the Caribbean. Oil tankers were the primary target, and losses of fuel supply at sea became so severe that a gas ration was introduced in Canada. The response of the RCN was swift. Corvettes from the WLEF were given new directives — protect oil shipments from the Caribbean to Canada. *Oakville* was among those ships that headed south in July 1942 to defend Allied fuel from U-boat attacks.

Her first assignment was to escort HA-1 (Halifax–Aruba), the initial convoy from the Caribbean to Canada. Aruba was a Dutch island with a sizeable refinery and was the transhipping point for all oil from the Lake Maracaibo oil field in Venezuela. Able Seaman Reg Adams noted the difference in convoy duty: "Our Caribbean convoys were a picnic after the Atlantic runs."[2] ASDIC operator Armour Weir recalls his first experience south: "Our first stop was Aruba, a parched-looking place, and all you could see was oil tanks and a refinery. I learned from an American solider that a U-boat had shelled the island that February."[3]

Members of HMCS *Oakville* posing for a photo in New York. (*Courtesy Keith Waddell.*)

HMCS *Oakville* in the Caribbean, 1942. (*Courtesy Edward Stewart.*)

Upon returning to Halifax, *Oakville* was again employed in some local escort duties before being sent on another HA series patrol. During this second convoy duty, *Oakville* was recalled to join a local convoy in the Caribbean Sea, TAW-15 (Trinidad, Aruba, Key West). During this local escort, *Oakville* was put to the test.

WOLVES IN THE CARIBBEAN — U94

The wolfpack was already well situated and prowling the warm and distinctly turquoise waters of the Caribbean by the time *Oakville* arrived to join TAW-15 in August of 1942. Back in August 1940, a 31-year-old Herbett Kuppish[4] was given command of a type VIIC U-boat. She was ordered on May 30, 1938 and was laid down September 9, 1939 at the Germaniawerft, a German ship-building company in the town of Gaarden near Kiel. Launched June 12, 1940, she was ready to be commissioned on August 10 of that same year, under the designation U94.

The VIIC was known as the "workhorse" of the *Kriegsmarine* and was produced more than any other type. It was a modified version of its predecessor, the VIIB; it was larger and heavier but had the same engine layout and power. She was thus slower than the VIIB but still a very effective weapon produced by the German navy from 1941 onwards. U94 was armed with five torpedo tubes — four positioned at her bow and one at her stern — which made her a force to be reckoned with, especially under the command of a seasoned captain.

Kuppish had been in the navy since 1933 and had risen to the rank of *kapitänleutnant* (lieutenant-commander). He was a rare breed, one of the few officers to serve exclusively in U-boats. Kuppish knew his craft, and before receiving command of U94, he had already led U58 on eight patrols and sunk four ships. By May 4, 1940, he had received both an Iron Cross 2nd Class and U-Boat War Badge. And his command of U94 would bring him even greater prestige.

After conducting training exercises, she left for her fist war patrol on November 1, 1940. On Decem-ber 2, U94 took part in the battle around convoy HX 90, and by the end of the month she had scored a total of six ships. On her second patrol, Kuppish and his crew sank seven more vessels, giving him a total of 13 ships sunk. His country recognized his actions by awarding him a Knight's Cross on May 14, 1941.[5]

In August he left U94 and spent a year on the staff of *Operationsabteilung* (the operational department U-boat tactical command). In December 1942, he served for six months with the high command of the *Kriegsmarine* and then took command of U847 in July 1943. A month later, while on her first patrol, U847 was sunk by aircraft from the escort carrier, USS *Card*. All hands were lost.

Taking over U94 was 24-year-old Otto Ites. Although very young, Ites had already gained much experience in U-boats. Joining the *Kriegsmarine* in April 1936, he was a member of the "Olympia-Crew," alias of crew 36, thus named for joining the navy in the same year as the famous Berlin Olympics. Not surprisingly, they chose the Olympic rings as their emblem. He served aboard torpedo boats *Kondor* and *Albatros* until October 1938, when he transferred to the U-boat force. He served in U51 and U48 before attending commander training and taking command of U146, which he left in August for U94.[6]

In September, Ites took U94 out on a North Atlantic patrol, in which he sunk four ships, including three from ON-14 (Liverpool to New York, Fast): British steam merchants *Empire Eland* under Master Donald Cameron and *Newbury* under Master Theodore Pryse OBE, and the Greek steam merchant *Pegasus*. Of the ships hit, only the crew of the *Pegasus* survived, and, although U94 observed that the crew of *Newbury* abandoned ship in lifeboats, none of the 38 crew, six gunners, nor Pryse, were ever found.[7] The fourth was the British steam tanker *San Florentino* under Master Robert William Davis, which was a straggler of ON-19. Although Davis, one gunner, and 21 crewmembers were lost, 31 were saved by HMCS *Mayflower* under Lieutenant-Commander George Stephen.[8]

From March to June 1942, while on his fifth and sixth patrols, Ites succeeded in sinking more ships along the American coast and from ONS-100 (Liverpool to Halifax, Slow), bringing him a total of 15 ships sunk. By August, he had received a Knight's Cross, on top of the Iron Cross 2nd and 1st class, and U-boat War Badge he had already received. Now an *oberleutnant zur* (lieutenant), he had grown popular with his crew and had earned their admiration. As Gaylord M. Kelshall elaborates: "All U-Boat crews wanted their commanders to have an element of luck and Ites had it."[9] Despite his young age, his crew referred to him as "Onkel Otto."

On August 3, 1942, he took his boat out of the 7th Flotilla base at St. Nazaire and met up with U463, a type XIV U-boat known as a "milk cow." It was about the same length as U94, but was built to re-supply the fighting U-boats in the Atlantic and carried only anti-aircraft guns for defence. Ites then received orders to operate in the Windward Passage, a straight between the easternmost region of Cuba and the northwest of Haiti that was popularly used by convoys. U94 reached its position on the twelfth and waited for news of a convoy sighting.

Oakville and her convoy were about to encounter an opponent who was no amateur, commanding a tried and tested vessel of war.

FIRST STRIKE

On August 24, 1942, the flotilla of ships formed up outside the Bocas del Dragon (Dragon's Mouth), a series of straights separating the northern part of the Golfo de Paria (Gulf of Paria) from the Caribbean Sea. It was to be the last convoy of the TAW series before being changed to the new TAG (Trinidad, Aruba, Guantanamo) route. It comprised 29 ships under the command of a senior officer in the destroyer USS *Lea*. The rest of the escort was made up of three RCN corvettes, *Oakville*, *Halifax*, and *Snowberry*; a Dutch gunboat, *Jan Van Brakel*; and three US Navy PCS (Patrol Craft, Submarine). Also, TAW-15 had continuous air support from No. 1 and No. 53 squadrons, which consisted of B18s and Hudsons — a shining example of convoys working closely with costal air force com-

mands, as Macdonald had explained months ago to the crowd assembled for *Oakville*'s christening.

The convoy route was as follows: TAW-15 would first head westward to meet with a group of oil tankers close to Aruba. It would then proceed to the Jamaican Channel, where ships from Panama waited. From there, the convoy would head to Guantanamo Bay, be joined by ships from the rest of the Caribbean, and then proceed to its final destination of Key West. At that point, another convoy from the Gulf of Mexico would merge with TAW-15, becoming a KN (Key West to New York) convoy. Once there, they would be further joined by American vessels and combine with ships from Halifax, whereupon the newly formed convoy would again change designations to HX. HX would then make the arduous journey along the North Atlantic Run, braving the frequently volatile seas to reach its final destination of England. *Oakville*, along with the other Trinidad based escorts, would only accompany the ships to New York. They were to then separate to escort another group of ships destined back south.

The dynamics of designing naval escorts was complicated, compounded by uncertainty and unexpected changes. As Kelshall observes, "It was a long and dangerous route and the planning and organisation involved thousands of people…. A convoy could become an administrative monster."[10] This was especially true when things did not go as planned.

Throughout the TAW-15 journey, the convoy suffered repeated attacks from German U-boats. The first occurred August 25 at 0437 in the morning. U558, under the command of 28-year-old Gunther Krech, a seasoned U-Boat commander who had already sunk 17 ships and been awarded an Iron Cross 1st Class and U-Boat War Badge (and later in September, a Knight's Cross), was on its second Caribbean patrol when it made contact with ships in the Jamaican Channel. Although not yet formed with the convoy, these ships were administratively considered to be part of the larger TAW-15 force.[11]

The *kapitanleutnant* eyed the small British freighter *Amakura*, a steam merchant under the command of Master Thomas Orford. Krech fired a single torpedo, which tore open the ship's hull, and the *Amakura* sank about 90 miles southeast of Port Morant. Thirteen crewmembers were lost. Orford, along with 25 crewmembers and five gunners, survived the attack, managing to make it to Point Morant Lighthouse.[12]

Krech was not aware that he had just attacked a ship that was part of a much larger escort force and was surprised at the quick response he received from a PBY (Patrol Bomber Consolidated Aircraft) Catalina, which plunged at the boat, forcing U558 to crash dive. More aircraft and a PC (Patrol Costal Ships) joined shortly thereafter, forcing Krech to leave before striking at the remaining ships.[13]

Later that day TAW-15 was struck again. U164, under the command of *Korvettenkapitan* (commander) Otto Fechner, a veteran officer with 18 years of service, discovered a group of ships south of Haiti. Just after noon, he set his sights on Master D.J. Boog's Dutch steam merchant *Stad Amsterdam*, which was having engine problems. Fechner fired two torpedoes at the ship laden with 4,000 tons of general cargo — one striking true, the other a dud, most likely due to U164's close proximity to the freighter. The ship stopped and slowly began listing to port. Fechner fired another torpedo to finish off the ship but missed. Three minutes later, he finally dealt the finishing blow, striking the aft section of the ship and sinking her by the stern. Thirty-five of the 38 crew managed to escape in two lifeboats and were questioned by U164, though the sudden presence of aircraft similarly took Fechner by surprise and forced him to flee. Both U-Boat commanders were unaware that they had in fact engaged a much larger convoy.[14] The battle of TAW-15 had begun.

On the 26th, convoy TAW-15 neared Aruba and was joined by the waiting oil tankers. The convoy then altered its course and headed northwest for the Windward Passage. Lurking roughly two miles away was U94. Ites quickly spotted the large convoy and dutifully assumed a shadowing position, trailing TAW-15 and reporting its position. U164, U511, and U558 all received the message and altered their courses accordingly.

The convoy continued on its way, long-ranged PBYs relieving the short-ranged A20s (Douglas A20 Havoc, Light Bomber). Although the U-boat commanders were unaware of it, Vice-Admiral John Howard Hoover's staff had also been alerted by U94's messages. Hoover was in command of the Caribbean Sea Frontier (CARIBSEAFRON) in Puerto Rico, whose mandate was to protect Allied shipping in the Caribbean Sea and Atlantic coast of South America.[15] CARIBSEAFRON had picked up the sighting report, as well as the attack summary sent earlier from U164 and U558. Headquarters was well aware of the threat facing TAW-15 and sent word to the convoy commander Lieutenant-Commander Clarence Broussard[*] in USS *Lea*. Although commanding a destroyer, Broussard was also a submariner and took the warning seriously. He ordered his warships to assume defensive positions around the convoy and readied themselves for potential attack.

By the 27th, the warships escorting TAW-15 were on guard as they neared the dangerous Windward Passage. USS *Lea* had taken a position to the fore of the convoy, with HMCS *Halifax*, HMNS *Jan Van Brakel*, and a USN PC on the starboard flank. HMCS *Snowberry*, another PC, and HMCS *Oakville* guarded the other flank, with *Oakville* stationed at the port quarter, 5,000 yards, 30 degrees from port column.[16] They were roughly four miles apart from the lead ship, and a solitary PC occupied the rear. These sheepdogs, along with the planes overhead, were keeping a keen eye for any sign of a surfaced wolf.

Later that evening, U511 made contact with the convoy and joined Ites. U511 was under the command of *Kapitanleutnant* Friedrich Steinhoff, an officer who had previously served on minesweepers and who had transferred to the U-boat force in 1942. Together they decided that the time to strike had come.

---

[*] Serving aboard the ship was an Edward L. Beach, who would later become a captain with over 10 decorations, including the Navy Cross. He is perhaps most famous for penning various books, including the famous *Run Silent, Run Deep*. Beach actually commented that Broussard ran "a ship beautifully" and that he personally visited Beach at submarine school.

OAKVILLE'S BAPTISM BY FIRE

Calm seas and full moons were a U-boat's worst enemy. The moonlight made it easier to spot the U-boat's silhouette on the surface, and with the addition of still waters, lookouts and aircrafts were better able to discern darker patches that could be enemy vessels. However, on the night of August 27, a cloudy sky kept the full moon largely hidden. Though brilliant when it shone, the drifting clouds seldom exposed the luminous sphere. In addition, the swells were heavy, Force 4 with whitecaps, which further decreased the escorts' ability to spot enemy vessels. Along with the humid heat that accompanied a typical Caribbean night, the ships were undoubtedly uncomfortable for the men trying to keep alert.

Oakville was zigzagging on course 351 true, moving steady at 8 knots. Trailing behind the convoy, Ites and Steinhoff took advantage of the hazy moon and moved to attack the convoys from the flanks, though they assumed different tactics. While Steinhoff had already encountered difficulties with Allied aircrafts, Ites had never faced opposition from the sky and thus was planning a more aggressive attack. U511 headed for the starboard side of the convoy, U94 the portside. Their approach was slow, diving continually to avoid attention from the PBYs above, but by midnight they had reached their desired destinations before the convoy.

Ites brought his boat almost to a stop and directed his bow back to the east, facing the merchant ships. The escorts were a good distance from their charges and he would have to slip past unnoticed to attack the freighters. Fortune was changing for Ites however: by 0110 GCT the sky had cleared and the light of the full moon now glinted off the water's turbulent, glassy surface. Though the swells made it difficult for the surface escorts to spot him, he would be fully vulnerable to the air. Unaware of the danger, Ites pushed forward.

HMCS *Oakville*, Caribbean Sea. (*Courtesy Edward Stewart.*)

U94 first passed HMCS *Snowberry*, positioned at the head of the port line. The U-boat moved slowly past the first guard, a US PC now before him. Ites was not concerned about the 80-foot craft, as it carried little firepower and posed little threat to his boat. His attention was instead focused on the barely visible bow wave to the PC's stern, which he knew was from another corvette — a vessel he had good reason to respect. Unlike the PC, this class of ship packed enough firepower to sink his craft.

HMCS *Oakville* was the last obstacle in Ites's path. Once he had passed the ship, he would have a clear run at the merchant vessels. His attention was likely focused solely on the corvette, and he therefore probably neglected to keep an eye on the clear skies above. Naval plane 92-P-6, a PBY-5A, was flying around TAW-15 in a continuous circuit. The pilot had actually not been scheduled to fly in the Windward Passage, but had received permission from his squadron commander to make an additional flight earlier in the evening. Searching for U-boats that were rumoured to be refuelling in the area, he came across one of the planes escorting TAW-15, approaching the Passage from the south. It had sustained a mechanical failure and was heading back to base. Naval plane 92-P-6 was immediately ordered to replace him, and headed for the convoy to perform escort duty.

At 0257 GCT, from an altitude of 500 feet, 92-P-6 spotted the darker shape of the fully surfaced U94 in the moon path, three miles astern the main convoy. The pilot did not hesitate, and dove for what he knew was an enemy U-boat. Ites's lookouts spotted the approaching PBY and alerted their commander. Ites immediately ordered the boat to make an emergency dive. Although he managed to submerge before the aircraft was overhead, the swirl and still-exposed conning tower proved sufficient targets for the pilot, who released four MK XXIX depth bombs, each with a 50-foot depth setting, from his racks. From an altitude of 50 to 75 feet they crashed into the water. U94 was on course 295 when the bombs exploded with enough force to launch four tall columns of water into the sky, which, combined with the thunderous echo, alerted *Oakville* to the U-boat's presence.

Depth charge exploding, as seen from aboard ship. (*Courtesy Edward Stewart.*)

Just prior to the explosion, Sub-Lieutenant E.G. Scott was on watch, the sole officer manning the corvette's bridge. With him was the usual compliment of deck lookouts, signalman, and a sailor in the wheelhouse. At this point, *Oakville* was zigzagging at 12 knots, steering 300 degrees true. The captain, Lieutenant-Commander Clarence Aubrey King, and the XO, Lieutenant Culley, were above the bridge, asleep under the awning above the compass shelter. The ship's remaining two officers, Sub-Lieutenant K.D. Fenwick and Sub-Lieutenant Harold "Hal" Ernest Thomas Lawrence, a 22-year-old English-born Canadian, were asleep below.

Oakville's captain had replaced Jones as the ship's CO on May 16, 1941. Jones had developed chronic seasickness and was drafted off, becoming a liaison officer for the West Indies. He would actually visit *Oakville* the same year in the Caribbean.[17] King, a fruit farmer from Oliver, British Columbia, was an experienced naval officer who had served with distinction aboard "Q-Ships" during the First World War. These were wolves in sheep's clothing — heavily armed merchant ships with concealed weaponry, meant to lure unsuspecting submarines into making surface attacks. Once the enemy vessel had revealed itself, the Q-Ships had the chance to fire and sink them first. King had been credited with one kill and two probable submarine sinkings. Before the end of the war he had reached the rank of lieutenant in the Royal Naval Reserve (RNR) and had been awarded a Distinguished Service Cross. Years later, in his book *Tales of the North Atlantic*, Lawrence would reflect upon his CO as "A real fighter-eater."[18] Able Seaman Reg Adams noted "Captain King was only aboard a short time when we heard the pipe 'Man overboard!' and everyone ran to the side to see who the silly bugger was who had fallen over the side. It had been a drill and, of course, we got hell from the captain for being stupid. The next drill was 'Fire in the galley!', but we were ready."[19] Clearly, this old sea dog was no stranger to naval combat, especially against submarines. It is no surprise, then, that King immediately rose, alert, and headed without delay to the bridge when the PBY's bombs exploded.

Scott and the lookouts spotted a column of water on the port bow, about a one-mile distance, and altered course towards it. He called for the CO, but the "old man" was already climbing the ladder to the bridge with Culley. King took command from Scott and ordered full speed ahead. He then had the boatswain's mate call in the gun crew, depth charge party, and officers. Shortly thereafter, the remaining officers appeared and took over their various stations — Scott on the gun, Fenwick on navigation in the wheelhouse, and Lawrence on the ASDIC. When the latter made it to his station, dressed only in his tropical shorts, he noted that Leading Seaman Hartman, *Oakville*'s senior anti-submarine rating, was already on set and sweeping. Culley was sent to roam between the various stations and stay off the bridge, perhaps a precautionary move by King to avoid having all his officers too centralized. Action stations were rung, and the engine room was informed that depth charges would soon be dropped.

The depth bombs dropped by the PBY had damaged the U-boat's diving planes, surface lights, and had forced the vessel to reduce its speed to 11 knots. The pilot spotted *Oakville* about a mile from the initial attack and started flashing "SSS" by Aldis lamp — the signal that a submarine was present. King and his crew could not yet see the enemy and a flare was released by the plane to illuminate the area, though it extinguished on contact with the water. Meanwhile, Lawrence had donned his headphones and, for the first time since his training at ASDIC school, heard the distinct sound of a submarine blowing its tanks. However, the PBY's attack had caused turbulence in the water, which prevented Lawrence from acquiring a good echo and reporting when to drop their own depth charges. He could only say that the U-boat was moving left. Annoyed but undeterred, King aimed his ship for the approximate spot of the flare. Once *Oakville* passed over the white foam left by the PBY's bombs, a five-charge pattern "B," set to a depth of 100 feet, was ordered released. Two depth charges left the corvette's throwers and three others rolled off the stern rails, splashing into the dark, glassy water and sinking. A moment after, a deafening explosion erupted behind the corvette, shaking the vessel and launching water high into the moonlit night.

Despite the damage it had sustained from the first explosion, Ites was still trying to submerge and hide his vessel when *Oakville* attacked. Various sources seem to argue about which blast actually damaged the U-boat's diving planes and tanks. Kelshall claims it was the blast from *Oakville*'s depth charges (which was why the U-boat was still, or at least partially, submerged) while other reports claim it was the PBY. Suffice it to say that after the corvette launched its 300-pound explosives, U94 had been damaged enough that it could not fully submerge. By this time, its equipment was shattered and the vessel had sustained cracks and leaks in its pressure hull. Ites knew that he had no other recourse but to fight. The PBY had continued circling above the area like a vulture, dropping flares to help *Oakville* spot the enemy and filling the night with the sound of its engines.

King ordered the ship to reduce speed to 160 Revs and altered course 30 degrees to starboard. At the wheel, Able Seaman Paul Faubert of Montreal answered immediately and skilfully manoeuvred the ship. Another depth charge pattern "B" was set, but before they could act Lawrence's voice came through the voice pipe. He had made contact — 10 degrees on the starboard bow bearing 335 degrees true, range 600 yards. U94 was now fully compromised.

King again ordered full speed ahead and altered the ship's course to match the bearing, which Lawrence reported was moving rapidly towards port. A minute and a half had passed — the crew's anticipation growing — when they heard, "submarine, on the port bow, less than 200 yards away."[20] The warning had come from Fenwick. Since the officer had just previously come on deck, he took the boatswain's mate call as a signal to go on watch and headed for the compass shelter. He had just signed the night order book and happened to glance out into the water when he spotted a German U-boat. U94 was about half a cable distance on the starboard bow, moving left and slightly opening. He was the first member of HMCS *Oakville* to spot Ites's vessel with his naked eyes.

Depth charge dropping into the ocean during a pattern. (*Courtesy Edward Stewart.*)

"Ho, ho!" King announced in "immense satisfaction."[21] At the news, Culley immediately went aft to the depth charges. *Oakville*'s captain then made a controversial move. Whether it was his training, past experience, or simple gut intuition, he ordered the ship to ram the U94. Although not unheard of — for ages naval officers have used the bows of their vessels as weapons — it was certainly not the safest tactic to employ. Kelshall notes in his book that during this period a destroyer had even been lost in the North Atlantic as a direct result of ramming a U-boat, and a corvette was a significantly smaller craft, its hull nowhere as dense as that of a destroyer. That being said, Captain Gus Miles's assessment of the U94 episode would note: "In my opinion, HMCS *Oakville* was undoubtedly correct in ramming the submarine to ensure his destruction."[22] Rear-Admiral G.C. Jones also agreed, adding, "The spirit and dash displayed by HMCS *Oakville* was worthy of the highest traditions of any service."[23]

At the command, *Oakville* quickly altered its course and prepared to strike the crippled U94. Signalman Milton Cheyne, an 18-year-old native of Montreal, fired two white rockets to illuminate and expose the U-boat. Culley ordered all crew to shore-up bulkheads as the corvette attempted to turn enough to ram the enemy. However, there proved insufficient sea room to perform the manoeuvre, and so the submarine passed under the ship's bow. King immediately ordered the helmsman to turn hard to port, causing the corvette to bump and scrape the length of the U-boat. The port .5's opened fire on the bow of the submarine, followed by the order hard to starboard in preparation for another ramming attempt.

In Lawrence's *Tales of the North Atlantic*, he notes an interesting anecdote that occurred around this time. In order to better view the enemy, King had moved to the starboard wing of the bridge, just as Cheyne, now manning the starboard side anti-aircraft machine gun, let off a stream of gunfire at the U-boat. He narrowly missed the captain's ear as King performed what Lawrence called a "standing side jump," leaping about 13 feet to the port side of the bridge for safety. Ironically, the move again put him in harm's way, as he narrowly missed another stream of gunfire

from his ship, this time from Signalman Bradley, who was manning the port-side anti-aircraft guns.[24]

When the range between the two vessels opened to one cable, one 4-inch round was fired, which narrowly missed U94's bow. Once in position to ram, all of *Oakville*'s guns opened up on the U-boat, peppering the enemy with fire from the Orlikon, 4 inch and .50-calibre machine guns, as the corvette sped forward on its second ramming attempt. Gunner Reg Adams, layer, was on watch when the PBY flares were dropped and called up the gun crew — loader, Gunner George Shiels; sight setter, Able Seaman Edward Davidson; and rammer, Ordinary Seaman George Lederman. Gunner Murchison Gordon was the gun captain who supplied orders to Adams, and Gunners Reg Cook and A. Johnson served respectively as the trainer and cordite supplier. Two more 4-inch rounds ripped at the enemy's conning tower and Ites ordered his gun crew to fight back with their main weapon — the 88-mm deck gun.

Ordinary Seaman Douglas MacLean acted quickly on the Orlikon and expertly raked U94's deck with gunfire — harmless to the U-boat's steel hull, but lethal to flesh and bone. As Ites's crewmen scrambled to man the 88-mm gun, they were instantly cut down. Ites ordered evasive action, increasing speed and completely surfacing his boat. This was his only chance: if he could hit the corvette with a well-placed shot from the 88-mm, he could significantly damage his nemesis and possibly escape. It was not to be. As U94 passed along the starboard side, Adams fired one 4-inch shell at the 88-mm deck gun, taking the weapon clean off the U-boat.[25] Just before *Oakville* struck, Ites reacted by swinging his boat to port, preventing the ship from making a clean hit. *Oakville* struck the starboard side of U94, which passed down the corvette's port side.

Leading Torpedoman Charlie Skeggs, in charge of the aft depth-charge crew, now saw an opportunity and didn't wait for orders from the bridge. Setting a single depth charge at 50 feet, he let if fall off the stern rail alongside U94. A heartbeat passed and then an explosion shook both ships violently. The bomb had exploded directly underneath the U-boat, severely reducing its speed. The proximity of the blast also affected the corvette — *Oakville*'s lights went

HMCS *Chaudiere* approaches a crippled U744, March 6, 1944. Although not U94 and *Oakville*, it does give a sense of how U94 might have looked towards the end of the battle. (*Courtesy Frederick Hall, National Archives of Canada.*)

out, black smoke spewed forth from her funnel, and phones immediately sounded on the bridge with various damage reports. The first call sought and received permission to free seaman Gowdyk from the flooding ASDIC compartment, but the second, which informed the bridge that the tiller flat was flooding, was denied permission to evacuate. Instead, they were instructed to commence immediate emergency repairs.

After the second failed ramming attempt, Culley had noticed the U-boat off the port quarter and moved from his aft position. There was a group of off-duty stokers standing around the fiddly, abaft the funnel, who were to assist in reloading the depth charge throwers. As the order to fire the depth-charge throwers had not been given, these men, keen to do their duty and attack the enemy, assailed the passing U-boat with a rather unconventional weapon of war — empty coke bottles, which were stored there by the canteen manager! Though their actions were certainly spirited, the XO redirected their efforts by quickly ordering

them below to arm themselves with rifles and pistols, perhaps sensing the possibility of a close-quarter engagement with the enemy. In the process, he secured a sidearm and a gas mask for himself before leading his men onto the fo'c'sle deck to the gun platform.

There was no escaping the inevitable for U94. *Oakville* ran out again, turned about, and bore down on the U-boat for the third time. This time *Oakville*'s bow struck true, and at 0345 (GCT) she rammed U94 abaft the conning tower at a nearly right angle. There was a loud crash, followed by the pulling and screeching of the two metal hulls as *Oakville*'s bow dug deep into U94 like a knife slicing into a tough loaf. It slid on top of the U-boat, and then over, forcing the submarine under its hull, which rose just under the stern.

With his ship's speed severely reduced, King ordered *Oakville* away from the U-boat. Faubert had nearly been thrown off his feet by the impact of the third ramming, but quickly regained his balance and answered his captain's orders. As he turned the ship about and, as directed by the bridge, brought *Oakville* back towards the crippled wolf, he distinctly recalled hearing his shipmates "cheering like mad"[26] after striking the U-boat for the final time.

U94 was finished — its pressure hull had suffered both numerous depth-charge attacks and gunfire from the corvette, and the ramming had smashed in the front of the conning tower and split the hull. King plotted his next move. Fenwick announced the "away boarding party" order on the captain's behalf, as his voice was much stronger and carried well. He then bellowed, "Come on, Lawrence, get cracking!" The young officer was instructed not to use the skiff to board the boat, which was the usual practice. Instead, *Oakville* would be brought right alongside U94. It was a risky manoeuvre, but Lawrence answered simply with "Aye, aye sir" and headed off.

Stoker Petty Officer Arthur Joseph Powell, a hard-rock driller from Timmins, was under the after gun platform when action stations had been sounded. He had served two years in the merchant navy and re-joined when the war broke out, eventually moving to the RCN in 1940. No stranger to shipboard life, he quickly ran up the fiddly, near the entrance of the stokehold, to standby the fire and repair party and to assume boarding party duties if called upon. He was dressed lightly in a pair of trousers, bathing suit, and a life jacket. When he heard the pipe ordering the boarding party to fall-in, he quickly threw on his cap and equipped himself with a pistol and flashlight.

MEN OF VALOUR

After the collision, Culley ran below to ensure that the ASDIC operator got clear of his station and to inspect any damage to the ship. King's move had struck a fatal blow to the enemy. Ites's boat was done. Yet, the corvette also suffered from the risky manoeuvre. The collision had given *Oakville* three distinct wounds: the ASDIC dome and oscillator were smashed, the ASDIC compartment had flooded, and No. 2 boiler room was quickly taking on water.

Culley was relieved to see that the ASDIC man had escaped his doomed station, but was troubled to find that the lighting plant had been damaged. In addition, the No. 2 boiler room was now flooding and the watertight doors had been secured to prevent the leak from spreading. All of the stokers had managed to clear out and were safe. Taking charge was Leading Stoker David Wilson RCN of Toronto, who was stationed in the No. 2 boiler room when the ship's plates were smashed and the room began to flood. Staying at his post despite the imminent threat to his life, he maintained control of the situation. Pressure was building in the boiler. If it blew, the explosion could further tear open *Oakville*'s plate and sink the ship. Stoker A. "Whitey" White quickly climbed on top of the drum to release the captured steam — a courageous move that posed significant danger to his own life and limb.

Boat being lowered from HMCS *Beaconsville*. (*Courtesy Harry Hollingsworth.*)

Before Culley moved to secure the emergency lighting and patch *Oakville*'s wounds, he went above to report the damages to the captain. Along the way he overheard a rating say that Lawrence and Powell had boarded the U-boat. He questioned whether the port boat knew that these men had boarded the submarine, and, guessing that the enemy boat might sink due to its wounds, ordered that the starboard boat also be launched to pick them up if necessary.

He continued to the bridge and reported to King, who quickly sent him back to supervise damage control. Bulkheads were shored-up with lumber to protect No. 1 boiler room and the engineering room, emergency lighting was quickly secured, and No. 2 boiler room was pumped out.

The boarding party had mustered on the forecastle. The 4-inch gun had suffered a misfire and was currently silent — a convenient place to prepare the team, it seemed. The .5's on the bridge were firing, and Ordinary Seaman Robert Drinkwater on the .303 Lewis gun was spurting rounds at the U-boat in quick, short bursts. The boarding party armed themselves with steel helmets, web-belts, .45 revolvers, grenades, torches, and a signal light for Cheyne. As they were all sleeping prior to the sounding of action stations, they were shoeless and shirtless, wearing only shorts or underwear — the better to bear the hot, Caribbean night. In addition to his kit, Lawrence also sported a length of chain to pass through the conning tower hatch and prevent the Germans from submerging their vessel.

Focused on preparing his team, Lawrence had not paid attention to the 4-inch gun crew working at their station. Having cleared the misfired round, they had now reloaded and had their sights trained on the approaching U-boat, which was now close to the port bow, where the boarding party had mustered. The danger became suddenly clear.

"Get down, get clear!" Lawrence yelled, throwing himself sideways as the 4-inch gun fired, the blast and sound of the powerful gun knocking Lawrence and his team unconscious. When Lawrence came to, he was in the break of the forecastle and had fallen eight feet. He was bleeding from his nose

and ears, and a quick survey showed that the rest of his team were still out. A voice and tap at his cheek caught his attention.

"Come on, sir, we're nearly alongside."[27]

It was Powell, who had come alongside to his position.[28] He had sustained a shattered eardrum from the blast but had remained conscious and had stripped off his pants and shoes, anticipating swimming to the U-boat. "Come on then, you can't live forever," Lawrence replied, and both men went to the side of the ship and looked down at the dark vessel below. Lawrence gave a quick glance to his second-in-command. "Going to go?" he questioned, and Powell answered, "Sure, I'm going to go." Though they were short members, they also knew they had little time to lose. Without another word spoken, and with only a gun and flashlight in hand, they jumped over the gunwale.

The landing was anything but pleasant. They dropped 10 feet to the U-boat's slippery, metal deck, Lawrence striking heel first. The force of the impact jarred his spine and snapped the elastic in his shorts, sending them to his ankles. He tripped over them and fell over the other side of the U-boat. He quickly recovered from the blunder, swimming back aboard the submarine along a swell. Unfortunately, aside from his gun belt and Mae West life belt, he was now completely exposed. Remarkably, Lawrence never mentions in his narrative that he felt at all embarrassed. Likely he was both focused on his task and keenly aware of the dangerous position he and his partner were in. Without further delay, they headed up to the U-boat's bridge. He gave but one order to Powell: shoot any Germans that he saw.

Suddenly, two Germans surprised Lawrence and Powell by exiting from an unknown hatch, while other crewmembers came from aft. Lawrence pistol-whipped the first with his .45, knocking the sailor overboard. The other crewmember jumped into the water after him. Both men had reason to be concerned. By this time *Oakville* was in the distance, its guns silent. It was just the two of them now against the rest of the U-boat crew, who were possibly armed and waiting to spring an attack. Lawrence knew that if the crew suddenly came out, he would have to check the rush of Germans to accomplish his objectives: capture the ship and acquire its codes,[29] ciphers, and intelligence. He and Powell rushed up the conning tower ladder to the bridge to find more Germans bolting out. Lawrence motioned them back and shot a red-bearded crewman who did not yield, while Powell shot another who was trying to exit the hatch. A third man quickly acquiesced and crouched down beside the hatchway, muttering nervously in German, while the rest of the crew stayed below.

What now? Lawrence thought as his brain raced.

Looking aft, he spotted a half-opened hatch. He at first thought that some of the U-boat's crew might flank him and Powell from this position. He reasoned he had to secure this area before proceeding. Turning to Powell, he told him to guard the bridge and see if he could gather any information from the Germans. He then proceeded back down the conning tower's ladder to commence his investigation.

The swells forced Lawrence to make his advance carefully. He rushed as the boat's hull rose and then fell prone, grabbing the deck's wooden gratings as it sunk again, waiting for the rolls to sweep over before repeating the process. In this way he reached the aft hatchway. Lawrence looked inside but was unable to make out any details in the darkness. Feeling pressed for time, he took a grenade and tossed it through the opening, hurrying back to the conning tower as it exploded.

Why at this time *Oakville* decided to repeat its antiaircraft gun assault on the U-boat was beyond both Lawrence and Powell. To Lawrence's dismay, rounds from his ship's pompoms started peppering the deck, forcing him to throw himself prone for protection. Bullets whizzed by, chipping away at the wooden gratings and lodging a wooden splinter in Lawrence's left arm. He took the pain as a cue to move and threw himself overboard and into the water to prevent being ripped apart by friendly fire. He waited in the water for the gunfire to subside before heading back to the submarine. Making his way back up the damaged conning tower, he met Powell. The conning tower's hatch, perforated by machine-gun fire from "Cheyne and Bradford"[30] and littered with broken coke-bottle glass (which took a toll on both men's bare feet) was also damaged and unable to close. Lawrence made his decision.

"Let 'em up," he ordered, "and see if we can get below."

Not surprisingly, none of the German crew stirred at the request — Lawrence and Powell *had* shot the first two who had tried to exit before. Lawrence's solution is worth recounting in his own words. He reports that he tried to lure the crew out by "… drawing on what Celtic charm I inherited from the Irish side of my family" and "crooned in dulcet tones down the hatch to the dark control room below."[31] At first they didn't move, which he later postulated was because he was holding Powell's flashlight to his face, which, with his bloodied ears and chest, must have been gruesome to behold. Lawrence placed his gun on the deck and said "Come on up. See — no gun."[32] His persistence did pay off, however, and shortly thereafter the crew began climbing up to meet them. Apparently they were eager to get out of the boat: "Up they came, and soon I found myself in a veritable mob."[33] Though neither he nor Powell seemed to realize it then, the first person to meet them was Otto Ites, wearing his knight's cross and limping; one of his legs was broken and the other had suffered three bullet wounds.[34]

To avoid being overwhelmed, Powell quickly escorted the prisoners aft, shoving and kicking the crew while waving his .45 and yelling "Marche!" Lawrence descended into the U-boat. About 22 to 23 Germans were now under Powell's charge. Before parting, Lawrence had again ordered him to acquire as much information from the prisoners as he could, so Powell did his best to communicate. He combined what little German he knew with English and blurted out: "*Du spracken Angleterre?*" One German came up and twice shouted "*Spracken zie Deutsch?*" while another followed with "English prisoner," stating it clearly while pointing at the deck. This caught Powell's attention and he tried to find out from the crew where the English prisoner was on board, but could elicit no further information. Another German spoke out and said "Bomb, bomb," again pointing at the deck. He knew that U-boats were equipped with self-exploding mechanisms and began to fear that they had set a "time bomb" below. He yelled two warnings down to Lawrence, hoping that the other heard him. He had to keep his concentration on the prisoners, who were speaking quickly and were made nervous by the rising water coming over the deck. The sub was sinking by the stern and the water had risen up to their knees. Still, Powell held his ground and kept his .45 pointed at them. In the back of his mind, however, he had plenty to be concerned about, especially that Lawrence had gone down below and was in the sinking vessel.

Once the Germans had been escorted off the conning tower by Powell, Lawrence entered the vessel. U94 was dark, and only the flashlight Powell had given him allowed him to see, though it was growing weak. Performing a quick survey for papers and intelligence, he discovered nothing of value and decided to head down another level to the control room. As his foot reached the deck it stepped into water, which, with the rolling of the vessel, rose from his ankle to chest in depth. He searched for the controls to the main ballast tanks. Slipping, he plunged underneath, thrown by a violent roll, and emerging disoriented. Finding the port side controls, he held onto a valve to steady himself against another roll, and spat out a mouthful of water and oil. Drawing on previous training, he searched for the nameplates, the dull orange light from his waning flashlight making the task exceedingly more difficult. He was studying the controls when a *thud*, followed by the shaking of the hull, caught his attention.

Lawrence knew what had caused the sound — a bulkhead had given way. The wave inside the vessel gained strength and crept up, twice forcing Lawrence to tread water before it fell to his waist. Then he heard Powell's voice: "Better get out, sir. I think they have a scuttling charge set." The news didn't surprise Lawrence, who had anticipated the move, but who had nonetheless been trying to keep that thought out of his mind. He was focused on his plan — if he could only blow the main ballast tanks and raise the U-boat, the captain would be able to deliver the rest of his boarding party along with Skeggs, who could disarm the bomb and allow them to capture the boat. However, finding the right levers was proving difficult and water was now coming through the open hatch he had descended. He noted another doorway with a wire half opened on it. Afraid that it was booby trapped, he left it alone.

He started to head above when he heard Powell's voice again, this time warning that an English prisoner may be aboard. Despite the danger, Lawrence headed back down to the lower deck, which was now rapidly filling with water. He performed another quick search but could find nothing. The U-boat was now rolling, and hung to port for a few seconds before moving back. He experienced a panic attack[35] as he realized how dire his situation had now become. Without delay, he darted for the ladder and started singing "Hail Queen of Heaven, the Ocean Star/ Guide of the wanderer here below,"[36] to keep up his morale as he ascended. Exiting onto the conning tower, he was greeted by pale moonlight and soft winds. He noted the red flames and smoke of a burning ship in the distance, and his own ship stopped and riding low in the water. He feared that she may be sinking but stilled this concern as he climbed down to meet Powell. "Couldn't find any papers," he told him. "Waters coming up, better get over-side." Drawing his gun out of its holster he motioned for the Germans to go over the side, which they eagerly did, swimming speedily away from the ship. "You too," he told Powell, who also jumped over the side.

In his book, Lawrence admits that he was saddened at this moment. He knew that the U94 was lost. She would never fly the Canadian White Ensign as his ship escorted her into Guantanamo Bay. Lifting his flashlight, he pointed it towards *Oakville* and began flashing "PSB, PSB, PSB" (please send boat), confident that one of the ship's signalmen — Cheyne, Bradley, or Ballinger — were keeping watch, keenly waiting for a signal. Without hesitation he received "T-T-T-T," indicating that the message had been received. A few seconds passed before he received his reply: "MRU" (much regret, unable).

Removing his revolver belt, he tossed it into the water and slung a pair of binoculars around his neck. For the first time he became keenly aware of his nakedness; jumping into the water, he performed single-armed backstrokes, certain to keep his other hand on his privates. Aware that sharks and barracudas frequented those waters (and the fact that his feet and arm had sustained wounds), he made sure that he swam in the middle of the Germans. Later, he would tell *Toronto Star* reporter Gordon Sinclair that he did this "… because if anybody was going to get cut up by sharks or barracudas, it wasn't going to be me."[37] He was also downright upset at losing the U-boat. When they were roughly 50 to 60 feet away, U94 finally succumbed to her wounds. At 0400 (GCT) her bow rose into the moonlit night and then sunk beneath the waves, 45 minutes after first being spotted.

THE CONTINUING CONFLICT

By this time USS *Lea* had arrived on the scene. *Oakville* contacted the lead ship and requested that it standby the boarding party. The following communications are taken from *Oakville*'s signal log and are in sequential order. They were transmitted by both radio transmission (talk-between-ships, or TBS) and blinker light, though it is unclear in which form each individual message was sent. The timing of each message is also unclear. Thus, using Culley's interview as a guide, I have endeavoured to place them where most appropriate.

> *Oakville* to *Lea*: "Close me."
> *Lea* to *Oakville*: "Am closing."
> *Oakville* to *Lea*: "Please close sub. Our boarding party on board."
> *Lea* to *Oakville*: "What is your target?"
> *Oakville* to *Lea*: "Sub rammed twice."
> *Lea* to *Oakville*: "Do you need assistance?"
> *Oakville* to *Lea*: "No."

Oakville's port boat approached, yelling "Lawrence, Powell!" into the night. They recovered their two crewmates and some of the 26 German sailors from U94. They had been swimming now for about half an hour and were tired. *Lea* was closer than *Oakville*,[38] and, seeing as their passengers were fatigued, the boat made for the American ship, which responded by reversing its engines to slow. A jumping ladder was tossed over the side of the destroyer to receive the occupants and

a chaotic gaggle of flaying arms and pushing bodies erupted in the boat as the panicked German sailors, desperate for salvation, struggled to reach the destroyer's ladder. Lawrence, annoyed by the display, shouted: "Gangway for a sub-lieutenant, we can't all be saved."[39] Despite the unruly conduct, both he and Powell, along with the Germans, made it safely aboard.

Lawrence's deportment was noted by the American crew. Since he was wearing nothing to identify himself as an officer, nor as a Canadian sailor for that matter, two large American sailors mistook him for a German and quickly seized him. As they started to move him off with the other prisoners, Powell and the boat crew from *Oakville* came to his aid and convinced them otherwise. Lawrence then reported to *Lea*'s Captain — in the nude no less — and decided to accept an invitation to have a shower and eat some sandwiches. Powell instead returned immediately to *Oakville*'s tender, which was towed by *Lea*'s motor launch back to the corvette.

Oakville had also managed to pick up the other German sailors in the water with its other boat, including the injured Ites. Harry Hollingsworth was aboard and immediately identified Ites by the iron cross around his neck. Ites was surprised by the size of the Canadian sailors, and commented, "Are all the Canadians sturdy chaps like you?", which the sailors acknowledged. Once aboard, the Germans started talking to the Canadians and seemed relieved to be prisoners.[40]

For them, the war was now over. Powell didn't stick around to chat — instead he went straight to his captain and gave a quick report.

"Good work, Powell." King replied after receiving the details. "Go below and have a drink."

Powell did as instructed and had a well-earned rum, but he couldn't stand idle and, despite his exhaustion, was soon assisting with repairs and shoring work.

Lea now contacted *Oakville*:

> *Lea* to *Oakville*: "Congratulations."
> *Oakville* to *Lea*: "Require assistance. Stokehold making water. Close in."
> *Lea* to *Oakville*: "Closing in. Can you steam under your own power?"

German Prisoners from U94. (*Courtesy Edward Stewart.*)

Oakville to *Lea*: "At reduced speed. Can you put our officer aboard?"

Lea to *Oakville*: "We are sending him back now."

Oakville to *Lea*: "We are closing you at slow speed."

Lea to *Oakville*: "Can you make port under your own power? We will rejoin convoy."

Oakville to *Lea*: "Good hunting."

Lea to *Oakville*: "Have reported your condition. Proceed slowly."

Oakville to *Lea*: "We will proceed at utmost speed with safety."

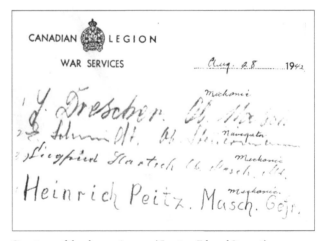

Signatures of the above prisoners. (*Courtesy Edward Stewart.*)

Oakville was done fighting. It was time for its crew to tend to their ship's wounds. Culley had taken all available hands from the upper deck and had them man the emergency pump. The intake was rigged in the flooded boiler room, and, after much effort, they finally managed to gain control of the flow of water coming in through the hole in the ship's bottom plates. The ordinary power pump was now able to control the flow, and the focus turned to building up steam in the forward boiler room.

Fire still flickered in the distance. The ship that Lawrence had noted when he exited U94 was ablaze and sinking. It was on the starboard side of the convoy, opposite from *Oakville*, the flames illuminating the night. While the escorts had been occupied with U94, Steinhoff in U511 made his advance. Fully surfaced, he launched four torpedoes at two ships and ducked back underneath the waves. The first pair was aimed at the large British steam tanker, *San Fabian*, under the command of Master Lloyd Guy Emmott. The warheads found their target, ripping through the side of the ship and igniting the 18,000 tons of fuel oil that was her cargo. Flames erupted with an explosive rumble, spewing fire hundreds of feet into the air. The large vessel quaked and began to sink. Thirty-one of the crew, as well as Emmott, abandoned ship before the inferno of wood and steel sunk beneath the waves, though 23 crewmembers and three gunners would not be as fortunate, and made the ultimate sacrifice. At 13,031 tons, she was the largest ship sunk in the Caribbean during the Second World War.[41]

Steinhoff's next two torpedoes were trained on the Dutch motor tanker *Rotterdam*. With equal precision, they struck the port side of the ship near the engine room. The 8,968-ton vessel immediately stopped and began settling from the stern. Survivors abandoned ship in lifeboats, later to be picked up by the American submarine chaser USS *SC-522*. Submerged, Steinhoff had one more attack up his sleeve. He fired two torpedoes from his stern tubes; they raced towards American steam tanker *Esso Aruba* under the command of Master Frank Pharr, the convoy commodore. One of them caught the ship on the port side between the No. 5 and No. 6 tanks, blowing a part of the deck 20 feet into the air and destroying pipelines. The engines and steering mechanisms of the ships remained intact, however. Regardless, the ship stopped and the crew prepared to abandon ship when the chief engineer reported that the ship

was still operable. Despite its damaged hull, and the threat of the ship breaking in two, it continued moving under its own power.[42]

The battle of TAW-15 had finally come to an end. Officially, it lost four ships totalling 27,766 tons, and two ships, *Esso Aruba* and *Oakville*, were damaged. For the Germans, the loss of U94 was a heavy blow. Nineteen of the crew died in the encounter and 26 were taken prisoner — plenty for the allies to interrogate and gain valuable intelligence from. The next morning, the Dutch ship *Jan Van Brakel* (*JVB*) contacted *Oakville*:

> *JVB* to *Oakville*: "That was a fine show of courage. Have you no casualties?"
> *Oakville* to *JVB*: "Thank you. No casualties."[43]

Oakville got underway at 0705 (GCT) on August 28, and was met shortly thereafter by HMS *Churchill*, which had came out from Cuba to meet the wounded ally. At 0755 she contacted the Canadian corvette:

> *Churchill* to *Oakville*: "Well done Canada. I have been sent to escort you in, but it looks as if you can still take good care of yourself."
> *Oakville* to *Churchill*: "Thank you. Our present maximum 12 knots. #2 boiler room about 10 ft of water, but we're holding it in check."

Oakville, wounded but victorious, arrived at the US naval base at Guantanamo Bay later that afternoon, at 1735 (GCT). For the next 10 days she would be out of commission as she underwent temporary repairs. *Esso Aruba* was purposely run aground to take the strain off its lower plates. Its cargo was removed and repairs started, though she would not see service again until February 1943. With them came the German prisoners and 59 injured survivors from the two sunken tankers. The Merchant Mariners told a fearsome story — they had been attacked by sharks before being recovered. Lawrence's concerns were clearly not unfounded.[44]

A NOTE ON SOURCES

Various sources — naval reports, newspaper accounts, witness statements, press transcripts and Lawrence's books, were utilized in creating the battle of TAW-15 narrative.[45] However, the various sources available regarding the U94 incident, including Culley, Lawrence, and Powell's witness statements, have unclear and conflicting information, some of which I feel warrant noting. For instance, Powell does not mention the incident with the 4-inch gun — only an after-note in his statement references the injury he sustained to his eardrum from the gun firing. He also explains that he and Lawrence were the only two to jump aboard the U-boat because they had guessed the correct side of the ship that would come alongside the submarine, the rest of the team having guessed the other side. In Lawrence's book, he explains that he and Powell were the quickest to react after the gun incident and were therefore alone aboard U94.

Culley and Powell both contradict each other regarding which side of the ship came alongside U94, a point noted directly in Powell's statement. Also, the dialogue in both Powell and Lawrence's statements differ at points, though they both generally have the same meaning.

Other sources, including the 2006 *Toronto Star* article written by Adam Mayers, raise points that Powell and Lawrence do not note in their interviews, nor Lawrence in his book. In Mayer's article, he mentions that after Lawrence ordered the Germans to exit the U-boat, a swell washed him overboard. Once he climbed back aboard, he fired his gun to ensure that it was still operable, which caused three Germans to jump over the side in fear of being shot. After this, Lawrence then entered the submarine while Powell stood guard and attempted to extract information from the prisoners.

Understandably, after such a traumatic event, some minor details could get confused or omitted. It is also natural that some people will tend to focus on some details rather than others. The main points of the incident, however, are not in question. Both Lawrence and Powell displayed great courage that night: boarding the U-boat, engaging the enemy in close quarters, capturing the vessel and crew, and escaping while trying to preserve their prize and acquire valuable intelligence to aid the Allied war effort. Unquestionably, *Oakville* and its crew are true Canadian heroes.

Emblem of U94, sunk by HMCS *Oakville*. (*Courtesy Edward Stewart*.)

HMCS *Oakville*'s crew, 1942. Back Row (Left to Right): A. Kerr, O.S.; C. Truss, A.B.; M. Blais, Ord. Sea.; C. Evans, O.S.; R. Wilson, Sto.; R. Browne, S.A.; A. Weir, L.B.; R. Chiswell, Ldg. Sto.; C. Waterman, Ord. Sea.; J. Hudon, Ord. Sea.; J. Tracey, A.B.; L. Knapp, Sto.; C. Gowdyk, A.B.; R. Drinkwater, Ord. Sea.; Second Row (Left to Right): G. Ballinger, Ldg. Sig.; A. White, Sto.; G. Shiels, Ord. Sea.; J. McNab, Sto.; F. Paquette, Sto.; D. Matheson, Sto.; M. Gordon, A.B.; C. Skeggs, Ldg. Sea.; G. Hartman, Ldg. Sea.; T. O'Callaghan, A.B.; D. McLean, Ord. Sea.; A. Allan, A.B.; G. Lederman, A.B.; P. Wozney, Ord. Sea.; E. Tissiur, Ldg. Sto.; J. Luke, A.B.; Third Row (Left to Right): W. Roberts, Tel.; A. Beer, Coder; L. Cook, A.B.; R. Bradley, Sig.; M. Cheyne, Sig.; W. Bond, Sig.; J. Ward, Coder; D. McKirdy, Tel.; C. Matheson, Tel.; G. Howard, A.B.; P. Faubert, A.B.; E. Davidson, A.B.; H. Love, Ord. Sea.; R. Adams, Ord. Sea.; H. Hollingsworth, A.B.; D. Wilson, Ldg. Sto.; Fourth Row (Left to Right): R. Howatt, Cook.; G. Tuck, E.R.A.; H. O'Flynn, S.P.O.; J. Dwyer, S.P.O.; A. Parr, C/E.R.A.; Sub. Lieut. E. G. Scott, RCNVR; Lieut. K. B. Culley, RCNVR (Executive Officer), Lieut. Comdr. C. A. King, DSC, RCNR (Commanding Officer), Sub. Lieut. K. P. Fenwick, RCNR, Sub. Lieut. H. E. T. Lawrence, RCNVR; A. Powell, S.P.O.; P. Hoy, E.R.A.; F. Harris, E.R.A.; N. Gent, S.B.O.; Front Row (Left): D. Corbett, Ldg. Tel.; R. Beardshaw, Sto.; A. Johnson, Ord. Sea., W. McQuaid, Ord. Sea.; Front Row (Right): G. Nanteau, Ldg. Sea.; S. Bennett, Sto.; D. Berquiste, E.R. (*Courtesy Edward Stewart.*)

CHAPTER 4
Faded Legend

ACCOLADES

For security reasons, knowledge of the event was kept censored and was not revealed to the public for three months. *Toronto Star* journalist Gordon Sinclair[1] published a multi-page article in the Tuesday, November 10, 1942 edition of the paper, which included interviews, pictures of the ship and crewmembers, and details of the event. Two proud mothers even appeared with their sons — Mrs. Agnes Love with her son Hugh, and Mrs. J.T. Weir with her son Armour — and Reg Adams, hailed by his shipmates as "The Best Shot in the Navy," appeared with his wife and daughter.

The Minister of National Defence for Naval Affairs, the Hon. Angus L. MacDonald, in a RCN press release reported that a:

> … submarine had been rammed three times during a relentless surface engagement, and that a boarding party from the attacking corvette, H.M.C.S. "OAKVILLE", had taken control of the disabled craft after brief resistance by the enemy

had been ended by the killing of two and the knocking overboard of three more.[2]

He went on to say that "This action … is one of which all Canadians may feel rightly proud, and I cannot commend too highly the heroism of the two men who leaped from the deck of their own ship to the deck of a German submarine in an effort to seize her if she were still seaworthy."[3] MacDonald stressed that the role the United States played in the affair was a "… striking example of the close partnerships" between the two navies and concluded that he felt proud in the "… spirit and dash displayed by H.M.C.S. 'OAKVILLE' and her crew."[4]

On Friday, December 18, 1942, MacDonald announced that three officers and seven ratings of HMCS *Oakville* were to receive awards for their heroism in the Caribbean. In all, one Distinguished Service Order, one Distinguished Service Cross, two Distinguished Service Medals, and six Mention-in-Dispatches were awarded. On the very same page, under the heading "Oakville Pleased Over Sea Awards," the mayor of Oakville remarked, "I think every one of them deserved it." Speaking of the awards made to their adopted crew, he added "I know it's not the right thing to say, but the people of Oakville would have been greatly disappointed if the crew had not been so honored." When asked if the town of Oakville was proud of their conduct in the Caribbean, he remarked:

> It would be silly to say we are proud of the boys. Everybody knows that already. The feeling that "the Oakville is our Ship" has spread throughout the town like wildfire until now everybody has it. Many feel that the crew are practically their own boys.[5]

This was the same man who had declared over a year earlier that "everyone in the district would be awaiting word of *Oakville*'s exploits." Their faith and hope were well founded. Who could have foreseen that in just over a year *Oakville* would again be making headlines for such a distinct and meritorious act? *Oakville* and its crew had raised the spirits of their community and delivered the hope that the town — and nation for that matter — so deeply needed. Naturally, they were ecstatic that their adopted "sons" were heroes.

The number of awards made to HMCS *Oakville*'s crew was greater than usual. However, King had actually recommended 17 crewmembers for recognition. As author Mac Johnston notes: "This figure, which did not include the skipper, was impossibly high as King, a World War I veteran, should have known."[6] That being said, one can find little fault in a captain nominating every crewmember he felt deserving of recognition.

Listed below are the recipients and their citations for each respective decoration as they appeared in the newspaper and naval press release:

Distinguished Service Order

Acting Lieutenant-Commander Clarence Aubrey King, DSC, RCNR

For skill, enterprise and resolution in a spirited and successful action against an enemy U-boat. Acting Lieutenant-Commander King was the commanding officer of HMCS *Oakville* when a U.S. aircraft indicated the presence of an enemy U-boat. After bringing the enemy into submission with depth charges, gunfire, and ramming, HMCS *Oakville*, by skilful manoeuvring, was laid alongside the U-boat, and a successful boarding of the enemy U-boat was effected in an effort to prevent scuttling. The keen judgement and prompt decision of Acting Lieutenant-Commander King contributed in fullest measure to the success of this engagement.

Distinguished Service Cross

Lieutenant* Harold Ernest Thomas Lawrence, RCNVR, HMCS *Oakville*

For gallant and courageous action in close contact with the enemy, Lieutenant Lawrence was in charge of a boarding party of two, which attempted to prevent the scuttling of a U-boat. With complete disregard for his own safety, this officer, accompanied by a petty officer, boarded the U-boat and, having subdued the enemy crew, he took action in an endeavour to prevent the scuttling of the U-boat, notwithstanding the fact that it was then sinking. His spirited and determined conduct was worthy of the highest traditions of the Royal Canadian Navy.

Distinguished Service Medal

Stoker Petty Officer Arthur Joseph Powell, RCN

For courageous action in close contact with the enemy. In a hazardous leap from his own ship to the deck of a German U-boat, Stoker Petty Officer Powell, one of a two-man boarding party, assisted in bringing the entire enemy crew into submission after a brief resistance. His coolness and efficiency in carrying out his duties onboard the enemy U-boat until she sank provided an inspiring example of gallantry.

Acting Stoker Petty Officer David Wilson, RCN

For meritorious services in face of the enemy. Acting Stoker Petty Officer Wilson was in charge of the boiler room when the compartment was flooded, owing to

---

* He had been promoted after the engagement with U-94.

damage caused by the ramming of an enemy U-boat. Remaining at his post throughout the action, Acting Stoker Petty Officer Wilson succeeded in controlling the danger of boiler explosion in the flooded section. His conduct throughout was marked by coolness, initiative and efficiency of a high order.

Mention in Dispatches

Lieutenant Kenneth Benjamin Culley, RCNVR

During the successful action of HMCS *Oakville* against an enemy U-boat, Lieutenant Culley displayed coolness in ensuring that full use was made of all the offensive weapons in the ship. He also displayed skill and energy of a high order directed to the speedy repair of the action damage.

Ordinary Seaman Douglas Thistle MacLean, RCNVR

Ordinary Seaman MacLean during a successful action by HMCS *Oakville* against an enemy U-boat, displayed great skill and resourcefulness in keeping up a heavy and accurate fire with an Oerlikon gun. His tenacity of purpose in manning the gun, despite stoppages due to defective ammunition, was worthy of commendation.

Acting Leading Seaman Charles Frederick Skeggs, RCNVR

In an engagement with an enemy U-boat, Acting Leading Seaman Skeggs of HMCS *Oakville*, in charge of the depth charge party, carried out his duties with coolness, skill and efficiency, and made a substantial contribution to the successful result of the action.

Engine Room Artificer, Third Class Alex McDonnell Parr, RCNVR

Engine Room Artificer Parr displayed coolness, skill, and efficiency of a high order in gaining control of action damage to the hull, sustained by HMCS *Oakville* after the ramming of an enemy U-boat. The conduct of Engine Room Artificer Parr throughout the action was marked by resource and courage.

Able Seaman René Faubert, RCNVR

During the ramming of an enemy U-boat by HMCS *Oakville*, Able Seaman Faubert carried out his duties as quartermaster, during an action lasting 45 minutes, with coolness, skill, and efficiency. The zeal and promptitude with which he obeyed swiftly moving helm and engine orders contributed to the success of the action.

Able Seaman Lloyd Murchison Gordon, RCNVR

Displaying coolness, skill, and efficiency in action while in charge of a 4-inch gun, Able Seaman Gordon, by promptness in bringing his gun into action in an engagement with a U-boat, caused damage to the enemy ship and thus made a substantial contribution to the result of the engagement.

Charles Gowdyk, an ASDIC rating whose station was at the bottom of the ship, went unsung. Reg Adams noted, "Nobody thought about poor Gowdyck until about a half-hour after it was all over and we rushed down to open the hatches and let him up."[7]

PROPAGANDA AND PUBLICITY TOUR

HMCS *Oakville* and her valiant crew were now national heroes. Lawrence and Powell drew special attention, becoming, as Mayers describes, "minor celebrities, feted in Toronto, Oakville and Brockville."[8]

From 1942–1943, they were sent on a publicity tour. Starting with a meeting in Ottawa with the Minister of the Naval Service, Angus L. Macdonald, they embarked on their journey, which included visits with the Port Arthur shipbuilders who constructed *Oakville* and even a stay in New York, where they were interviewed on radio and met the Mayor Fiorello LaGuardia as his personal guests.

A slew of publicity shots were taken along the route, including pictures of both men visiting sites in New York City, of Lawrence at St. Clare's school in Toronto, and, of course, of both men with residents of the Town of Oakville. The town held another ceremony, this time to honour the two heroes, which many in the community went to observe.

Hal Lawrence and Arthur Powell. (*Courtesy Edward Stewart.*)

Arthur Powell shakes the hand of Angus L. Macdonald with Hal Lawrence observing. (*Courtesy Edward Stewart.*)

Powell and Lawrence meeting Mayor LaGuardia in New York. (*Courtesy Edward Stewart.*)

Lawrence visits students from his old elementary school in Toronto. (*Courtesy Edward Stewart.*)

(*Above*) Visiting ship-builders in Port Arthur, Ontario. (*Courtesy Edward Stewart.*)

(*Left*) Powell and Lawrence in New York. (*Courtesy Edward Stewart.*)

(*Left to Right*) Stoker Petty Officer A. Powell; Mrs. Powell; President of the Robert Simpson Company, C.L. Burton; and Lieutenant H. Lawrence. (*Courtesy Edward Stewart.*)

Lawrence and Powell have dinner with the mayor of Oakville. Note: *Oakville*'s bell is displayed on the table. (*Courtesy Edward Stewart.*)

Lawrence addressing a crowd in Oakville, Ontario. (*Courtesy Edward Stewart.*)

Men of Valour poster. (*Courtesy Oakville Museum.*)

However, their fame, as well as that of the ship, was perhaps best embodied in a war propaganda poster.

All around Canada this poster was circulated. Its slogan, "Men of Valour, they Fight for You!", is presented with an image of Lawrence and Powell on U94, engaging the U-boat with HMCS *Oakville* in the distance. Note that the picture, understandably, does not depict Lawrence in historically accurate attire.

With all the publicity and hype, *Oakville* and her valiant crew were starting to approach legendary renown.

AFTER U94

After her temporary repairs were finished, Oakville was not yet ready for the high seas until the new year, when she resumed escorting convoys between New York and Guantanamo Bay. The U-boat offensive in the Caribbean had greatly diminished, and in March,

Stokers assist Chief Engine Room Artificer (ERA) Alan Parr, who is cleaning and servicing the anchor winch. (*Courtesy Allan Mole.*)

(*Left to Right*): ERA Frank Harris, ERA Allan Mole, Chief ERA Alan Parr. (*Courtesy Allan Mole.*)

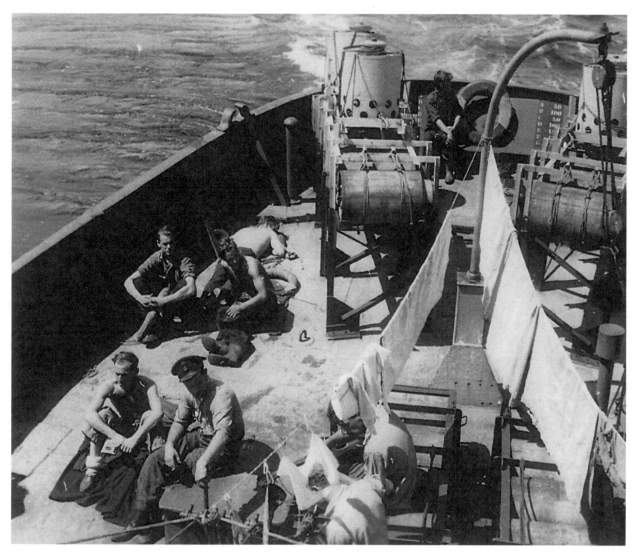

Laundry day aboard *Oakville*. (*Courtesy Allan Mole.*)

Oakville returned to Halifax for an annual service and to have her armament refitted. She again returned to WLEF, resuming escorts between New York; St. John's, Newfoundland; and Halifax. Things were pretty routine for *Oakville*. Jack Drysdale, an able seaman aboard *Oakville* and an ASDIC operator from 1942–1943, recounted: "I think *Oakville* lost more domes than any other ship in the navy. If she wasn't striking logs, she was shearing them off in the ice packs outside Newfie."[9] Author Mac Johnston elaborates, explaining that: "Corvettes, being bare-bones vessels, did not have retractable domes, which meant that many were sheared off."[10]

On December 15 of that year, she reported to Galveston, Texas, to have her fo'c'sle extended, radar updated, machine guns replaced by singly mounted 20-mm Oerlikons, and a new hedgehog installed that would throw anti-submarine mortars ahead of the ship. The updates would take until March 29, 1944, to be completed, after which she visited Halifax before undertaking working-up exercises at Bermuda to prepare for further operations. On June 16, 1944, she returned to WLEF and continued faithfully escorting convoys, tirelessly moving up and down the routes.

(*Above*) HMCS *Oakville*'s crew, 1943. Note: the sailor above Hal Lawrence is holding the ship's mascot, a cat (unfortunately I have not been able to find mention of its name).[11] *Back Row (Left to Right):* C. Llewellyn, A.B.; C. Richardson, A.B.; W. Bayliss, O.D.; R. Humphrey, Sto. 1; R. Burton, A.B.; M. Benson, O.D.; D. Woods, Sto. 2; G. Brickenden, O.D.; R. Boyles, A.B.; W. Goss, O.D.; N. Myke, A.B.; P. Faubert, A.B., J. MacFarlane, O.D.; S. Bennet, Sto. 1; W. Sargent, Ldg. Tel; J. Smith, Ldg. Sto.; J. Purdy, A.B.; *Second Row (Left to Right):* L. MacDonald, Sto. 1; W. Hodges, A.B.; J. Llewellyn, A.B.; W. Einarson, O.D.; A. Coutts, Sto. 1; H. Aubin, Sto. 1; H. Harris, O.D.; J. Whitehead, Sto. 1; A. Price, Sig.; O. Martin, Sig.; M. Cecchini, Sto. 1; M. Piperski, Sto. 2; J. Drysdale, A.B.; J. Dunn, A.B.; A. Brooks, O.D.; J. Hudon, A.B.; G. Lederman, A.B.; H. Hollingsworth, A.B.; J. Carriere, Ldg/Sea.; *Third Row (Left to Right):* W. Keirnan, Stwd.; R. Middleton, CK(S).; B. Mitchell, Sig.; J. Kartecaner, Stwd.; J. Ward, Cdr.; J. Smillie, Cdr.; R. Coy, Ldg/Sig.; D. Weaver, Cdr.; D. McKirdy, Tel.; A. White, Sto.1; J. MacDonald, O.D.; A. Moore, Ldg/Sto.; G. Rakuson, A.B.; L. Garner, A.B.; C. Mathewson, Tel.; E. Clarke, L.S.A.; C. Skeggs, Ldg/Sea.; T. O'Callahan, A.B.; G. Sylvain, A.B.; H. Low, L/S.B.A.; E. Cudmore, A.B.; *Fourth Row (Left to Right):* D. Jackson, C.P.O.; F. Harris, E.R.A.3; D. Wilson, S.P.O.; J. McDonough, E.R.A.4; K. Kraeling, P.O.; A. Parr, C/ERA 3; S/Lt. R. Peel.; Lt T. Young; Lt. H. E. T. Lawrence X. D.; Lt. H. F. Farncomb, C.O.; S/Lt. K. D. Fenwick, N.O.; S/Lt. A. D. Russell; S/Lt. J. A. Martin; R. Rimmer, P.O.; J. Robinson, E.R.A. 4.; E. Tisseur, S.P.O.; R. Sewell, S.P.O.; A Mote, E.R.A.4; P. McKeown, Ldg/Ck. *Front Row (Left):* C. Truss, O.D.; W. Roberts, Tel.; A Graham, O/Sig.; A. Allan, Ldg/Sea. *Front Row (Right):* G. Shells, A.B.; W. Gillis, O.D.; R. Bentham Ldg/Sto.; J Noyes, A.B. (*Courtesy Edward Stewart.*)

P.J. McKeown holding *Oakville*'s mascot. McKeown, on the back of the photo, notes: "Here is the mascot cat that … I had forgotten about." (*Courtesy P.J. McKeown.*)

Jack Russell. (*Courtesy Jack Russell.*)

JACK RUSSELL INTERVIEW

I pick up the phone on a November evening. It's a few days prior to Remembrance Day, the weather grey and dreary, and I can't help but note the importance as I dial Jack Russell's phone number. Since Joe Smyth's passing last year, Jack is conceivably the last living person to have served aboard HMCS *Oakville*. His son, Larry, gave me a warning along with his father's number: "he is extremely hard of hearing and often has difficulty hearing and conversing on the phone unless he has prepared and taken steps to reduce the extraneous noise around him."

This is the first time I have spoken with Jack since the Naval Centennial Celebrations in Oakville (which I will cover in a later chapter). He, along with Joe Smyth, were both front and centre during my speech on HMCS *Oakville*. I recall how proud Jack was to lead

the parade and, despite some difficulty walking and the concerns of his family, how he insisted on marching. I recall with even greater clarity his eyes, observing me keenly as I spoke to a crowd about the history of our town's namesake ship — his ship. With so many veterans of the Second World War "crossing the bar,"[12] to use the naval slang for the death of a sailor, I pause for a moment to let the importance of what I'm about to do sink in. I have no idea what Jack will remember from his time aboard the ship — the amount of clarity and detail he will be able to draw out for me — but I am thankful for the chance to speak to the old salt.

I dial his number and remind myself to speak loud and slow.

Jack picks up the phone quickly. I introduce myself and am relieved when he recalls me: "Ah, you're the Officer who talked at the Museum … the young fella with the beard. John, right?" I smile, let him know he's close on the name, and that I would like to ask him some questions about HMCS *Oakville*. He laughs a bit, warning me that he is not certain how much he will remember, but will be glad to speak.

I soon realize that Jack's memory of the war, and especially the ship in which he served in, is remarkably clear.

I start by asking him about the first time he saw the ship.

Jack Russell had just turned 18 when he signed up with the RCNVR. He was stationed at HMCS *Stadacona*[13] in 1943 and had just completed his torpedoman's course. He was eager to get on a ship, a sentiment that was shared by all his peers. After all his time training and preparing, he wanted a chance to finally put his skills to good use.

As he recalls, his orders came quickly: "Before I knew it, I was told I was to be on the *Oakville* tomorrow." He was told that the ship was headed to Galveston, Texas, for a re-fit and fo'c'sle extension. The name was already familiar to Jack — it had been in all the papers and just about everyone in the fleet had read about its encounter in the Caribbean. His mind played over the details of HMCS *Oakville*'s gritty battle, of Lawrence and Powell's daring capture of U94. He was both honoured and glad to be chosen to serve aboard such a ship and looked forward to joining its crew the following day. However, his first impression of the ship was to be rather lacklustre.

The next day he went up to the jetty, and for the first time his eyes beheld the famed corvette. His gut cringed with disappointment. As he recalls: "My first thoughts were that it looked pretty ancient-like," quickly adding with a light chuckle, "and I thought it needed a paint job." It took him a bit off guard, the hype and galvanizing in the papers perhaps blowing his expectations out of proportion. *Oakville* was, after all, still just a lowly corvette. It was instantly clear to him that she needed some repairs and, upon closer inspection, that the ship still bore scars from what must have been her fight with U94.

And it was with that realization that something within him stirred. He suddenly beheld the ship with new eyes, as if seeing it only now for the first time. The scars, dents, rust and grime transformed into badges of honour and marks of strength. *Oakville* had clearly been tried, tested and ultimately proven herself a fighter. "It certainly looked like a gritty warship," he concluded, the pride clearly evident in his tone. He remembers reaching out and touching her hull, feeling privileged to have been chosen as part of her crew.

Unbeknownst to him at the time, it would be the only ship he would serve in during the war. *Oakville* would be his home for the next few years.

Jack never met Lawrence, Powell, or King — pretty much the entire crew had been granted leave or transferred by that time. In fact he only knew one sailor who was on the ship during its battle with U94 — Harry Bains. Jack knew Harry back from his hometown of Petrolia,[14] a small town near Sarnia, where he was born. Harry was in charge of the local beer store. As Jack recalls, he never spoke much of the ship's battle with U94: "it never came up much and I thought better than to ask."

Jack proceeds to tell me what it was like aboard the ship and does not spare the gruesome details of his seasickness (which I added to chapter 1). He remembers the ship arriving at Galveston, Texas in December of 1943 for its much-needed refit. His

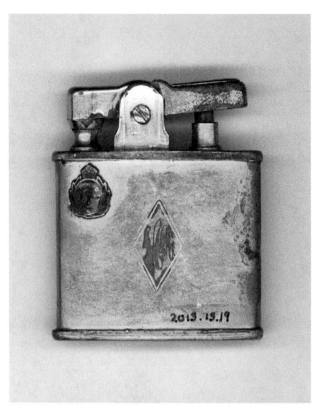

Front of the lighter given to each sailor aboard HMCS *Oakville* by the town of Oakville, Christmas 1943. (*Courtesy Oakville Museum.*)

Opposite side of the lighter. (*Courtesy Oakville Museum.*)

voice warms at this point and he starts to laugh —
his time in Texas is one he remembers very fondly:
"we had Christmas in Texas. We ate a Christmas
mess dinner and received a gift from the town of
Oakville." Jack's gift was a silver, zippo-style ciga-
rette lighter. On one side was inscribed H.M.C.S.
OAKVILLE and, on the other, the RCNVR crest.
It was, as he explains, a good gift, "as everyone
smoked; cigarettes were only 5 cents a package you
see." It was also something he cherished and kept in
good working order for his whole life.

"The Americans were good to us," he adds, after
talking about his gift. While the ship received its mod-
ifications, Jack met a family down in Galveston that
took him under their wing "like a mom and dad would."
He was given a room to stay in, and they also had a
daughter that was near his age who he went out with
a few times to catch a film and walk the town. "We
were just friends," he explains, and although he does
not remember much of their conversations, they were
nice times.

During the week the crew would work on the ship
but had plenty of spare time, including weekends off.

Jack remembers a few outings with his shipmates
to Houston, which was always an enjoyable time.
Once the fo'c'sle extensions were completed, they finally gave the ship the fresh coat of paint it so direly
needed. Jack also tells me that everyone helped with
the repairs, "didn't matter the rating."

But their time of leisure and comfort in Galveston was not to last — the ship was ready for sea, which
meant it was also time for HMCS *Oakville* and its crew
to get back to the war. She set sail to Jamaica for workups, or as Jack calls it, "playing navy," where they played
war games with other ships, underwent manoeuvres,
and put the ship and crew through their paces.

Jack explains that the other, older, crew was given
28 days leave, so *Oakville* essentially was being crewed
by green sailors, and it was necessary for them to not
only test the new ship, which now had the elongated
fo'c'sle and new weapons, but to teach the crew how
to do their job. He recalls appreciating having more
room in the ship for off-duty and sleeping — the refit
had made a noticeable difference to the ship.

Oakville's 4-inch gun plus ratings posing for a picture. (*Courtesy Robert Waddell.*)

HMCS *Oakville*, after receiving its fo'c'sle extension. Note the placement of the mast, now behind the bridge. (*Courtesy Edward Stewart.*)

Jack suddenly lets out a hardy laugh, which takes me a bit off guard.

"What's so funny?" I ask him.

"I was just thinking of something that happened down when we were in Jamaica," he answers. "I'm going to tell you something, and you may think 'how can that be real,' but I'm telling you the honest to God truth."

Naturally I'm intrigued and encourage him to tell me the tale. As part of their workups, he explains, it was required of everyone aboard ship to jump overboard and tread water for a certain length of time.

Seems reasonable enough to me, so I'm not catching on to why he's laughing again.

"I couldn't swim!" he confesses.

"You're kidding?" I question him, but he just laughs louder.

"Nope, never learnt."

"But didn't you have to learn, or pass a swimming test, in your basic training?" I prod. Jack proceeds to tell me what he feels is the real unbelievable part to his story. He took his basic training in Windsor, Ontario, and they would utilize the local YMCA pool for swim training. However, every time they were scheduled to head to the YMCA, he just happened to be sick that morning (and he swears that it is entirely a bizarre coincidence — he was not pretending nor trying to avoid it). As a result, he never learnt and still, to this day, cannot swim.

"Weren't you worried about not being able to swim if you fell overboard?" I ask. Jack simply answers, "If I fell in the Atlantic, I figured being able to swim wasn't much use. It would just prolong the inevitable — better to get it over with."

But now Jack was aboard *Oakville* in the Caribbean, and had to jump into the water and swim with the entire crew. He remembers thinking, "Well, I can't swim, but if this lifebelt is as good as they say it is, I'll buckle it tight and jump in with the rest." So he approached the side, peering at the multiple bobbing heads, carley floats, and whalers, held his breath and jumped in.

Swimming party during workups in the Caribbean. Note: the sailor wearing his life preserver. (*Courtesy Allan Mole.*)

Luckily for him, the navy was right about the effectiveness of their lifebelt. He tread water for a few minutes, and then was scooped up into one of the floats. He made a point to never get into the water again.

Jack chuckles, "And I never learnt to swim — I can still drown in a couple inches of water."

He then adds as an aside that they had to pull the whalers and carley floats up by hand. It was gruelling and taxing work to lift the vessels out of the water and put them back in their respective places — like a tug of war with a boat, as Jack describes it. Fifteen to 20 sailors would pull a line affixed to one end of a whaler, while another 15 to 20 would pull the line affixed to the other. The hoisting was "very hard work — no electricity, winches or anything. All just hard labour."

OAKVILLE'S CLOSE CALL

"What was your most memorable moment aboard *Oakville*?" I ask Jack. "What stood out the most?"
I hear Jack make some sounds, mulling over the question. Although I don't know what he will tell me, I assume it will likely be something to do with the hours, watch system, or weather. For that reason I am completely caught off guard by his answer.

"I guess the time we nearly got hit by a torpedo," he says.

Did I hear him right?

"Torpedo — what torpedo?"

"Oh, it's nothing, really," he tries to reassure me. "Not worth writing about."

I smile to myself. Jack, like most veterans I've spoken to, is humble and avoids trying to sound heroic or grandstand when talking about his past war experience, but I also know that there's more to the story. So I prod further and, with some encouragement, he decides to tell me about the close call with the torpedo — another piece of HMCS *Oakville* brought back from the lost annals of time. And, as I soon realize, it's a story that's far from being "nothing."

It was 1944, as Jack remembers it, and the memory is still clear in his mind: "like it happened yesterday," he says. *Oakville* was somewhere between Halifax and St. John's, escorting ships in the usual zigzagging pattern that was customary for convoys to follow. At this point the ship was already a veteran of this kind of duty, and aside from stomaching rough weather there was not much action for the crew on these runs.

Jack was on watch that night, and though he doesn't recall the date, he does remember the weather being mild and the waters calm. It was sometime in the summer.

"Being on watch, you dressed to what the weather was like," he explains. "If it was rough, then you wore your Mae West life jacket. In the winter we had nice long slacks and boots." What sailors wore depended on their captains — some would require sailors to be in their dungarees, coat, and hat, while others allowed the crew to wear non-uniform clothing when out to sea.

This night, he was lightly dressed. He was standing with his binoculars, scanning the darkness for anything that seemed amiss. Despite the visibility afforded by the clear skies, there was not much he was able to see. The convoy was so large and spread out that he was not able to pinpoint another ship on the horizon. Jack tells me:

> When you're on watch duty you looked out to the surface of the water as far as you can see, scanning continuously, ahead of you if on the bridge, but if near the stern, where the pom pom gun was, you kept an eye on the water. You were looking for a sub that had surfaced, or a periscope, and had to be prepared to call a warning and let the officers know, who would then call action stations.

It is a sentiment that David Francis Stewart echoes from his experiences at sea:

> You were always watching. You could go to sleep on your feet but you'd get in deep trouble if you were caught.

It was draining work — you felt as if you were always being shot at. Every minute of the day you felt someone was taking a shot at you, so you had to stay alert. As you got close to Europe you'd also keep your eyes open for adrift mines. We would shoot at them with rifle fire or machine guns — they never exploded, oddly enough, just would sink.

For hours Jack had been scanning the black waters, glinting with specks of moonlight, and, as usual, he had nothing to report. He wasn't even confident that he would notice a periscope poking through the waves, let alone a surfaced submarine. It was long and tiring work, trying to remain vigilant and fighting off the sheer boredom and fatigue of scanning continuously over waters he could barely see. It could be pretty frustrating too: "It was kind of difficult in the dark, just using the light of the sky," Jack explains. His frustration was shared by all sailors. Stewart remembers that "at night you couldn't see anything," and that "you didn't like a moonlit night because you were a sitting duck. Sure, you could see better, but so could the U-boat."

Electric lights were not allowed at night. *Oakville*, along with all ships in the convoy, was trying to avoid making herself an easy target for U-boats. They even had blackout curtains on all the hatchways. As Jack remembers, "when you opened a hatch, there was two or three blankets obscuring the entrance in which you had to walk through." They were spaced a few feet apart from each other so that when you negotiated past one blanket, another would be either in front or behind you and prevent the light from within the ship from spilling out. In the dead of night, even the subtlest flash of light could stand out at sea and catch the attention of the enemy, who was most certainly out there. And, once in a while, the enemy liked to send not-so-subtle reminders of its presence.

It was 0400 when his watch finally ended. He handed over his binoculars to his relief, and having nothing to report (which had become routine by this time), decided to head for the nearest hatch and swing by the galley. Hopefully he could get himself a piece of toast with jam and a hot beverage before trying to squeeze in some sleep prior to breakfast and his next duties. He had just put his hand on the latch when he heard the starboard lookout yell into the voice pipe that a torpedo was in the water approaching the ship's starboard bow.

Jack recalled wondering whether he had heard the warning correctly.

Despite the dark, the clear skies provided just enough light for the starboard lookout to see the white trail left by the torpedo's screw as it raced, only a few feet under the water's surface, towards the corvette's bow. Thankfully, the sailor did not second-guess what he saw and immediately sounded the alarm. Likewise, the OOW was also on his game, and without hesitation, ordered the helmsman to turn the ship hard to port. *Oakville* lurched suddenly and tilted, Jack balancing himself as the ship made the quick evasive manoeuvre. At that moment he knew he had heard things correctly. He held his breath, bracing himself for an explosion, but the torpedo missed. As the starboard lookout would later recount, he saw the torpedo parallel to the ship — as if the two were racing on a track — and an instant later the torpedo was gone. It was almost close enough to hear.

Action stations were called and alarms sounded. The snack would have to wait, Jack realized, as he raced to the port side of the ship to his station at the depth charge thrower. Another torpedo trailing behind the first also streaked past *Oakville*, its trail disappearing into the night.

"That really smartened us up," Jack explains.

As *Oakville* had already proven, it was not the ship to flee from an attack. Instead, "the ship monkeyed around," heading straight for the direction the attack came from.

Jack arrived at his destination and was greeted by two sailors who were also part of his station. The other men were responsible for loading the thrower while Jack was tasked with setting the charge and firing the explosive. A cursory glance at each other's eyes relayed more than words could do at the moment —

they were all scared. This was no drill: the enemy was out there and had nearly destroyed the ship.

"I mean, that could have been it for us," Jack explained, "but you're in the middle of the ocean so what could you do?"

Their feelings would have to wait — they had a job to do. Orders were already starting to come through the voice pipe as *Oakville*'s engines pushed the ship into the dark. The ASDIC operator was relaying information to the OOW, who in turn was sending information to Jack at his station, telling him the depth to start setting the charges. His two partners began hauling the heavy charge up to the launcher while Jack took his instructions from the bridge. Once the charge was in place, he used a key to set the depth at which the canister would sink and explode.[15]

"You were supposed to be able to tell the depth by the click," Jack tells me. "The first click was 50 feet, the second 100, but when you're out there and it was a bit rough, you couldn't always tell and get the click right. Sometimes they would be a bit deeper and other times shallower."

He set the charge to 50 feet and waited for the order to start their first pattern, which would consist of launching about 10 depth charges. In sequence, the starboard side of the ship would also launch explosives, as well as the aft, which would let the charges roll off the rails. *Oakville* was about to retaliate in full force.

Jack and his team had no clue if the ASDIC operator was getting a signal or not, but the order to attack came. Jack fired the first charge. It launched high into the sky and safely away from the port side of the ship, the sound of the drum splashing into the distance mixed with the lapping of water against the hull. The briefest of moments passed before the air around them exploded with heavy detonations. Behind, and trailing on both sides of *Oakville*, geysers erupted and spewed water and spray high into the air.

"They could be set to be explode at 50, 100, 125 feet — and sure enough, at that depth they would explode," Jack tells me. "At 50 feet you got a pretty good jarring from the explosion and could even get some spray from the blast. The deeper you set the charge, the less action on the ship."

Jack and his team did not pause to take in the site, nor did they let vibrations of the explosion or the water splashing on the deck deter them. This is what they had trained for — rehearsed time and time again through countless drills. As they had practiced, they performed their dance, deftly hauling the second charge into place. Jack set the depth and fired the second charge into the night.

Orders came through the voice pipe to make adjustments in depth. Jack would use the key, clicking the charge to the appropriate depth, and resume firing. *Oakville* steamed ahead, strategically carpeting the water in its wake with explosion after explosion. After the first pattern was done, the ship changed course and retraced its steps, the bombardment continuing with haste. Jack adjusted the depth — 50 feet, 120 feet, 200 feet, 100 feet — in what became a rhythmic cadence of set depth, fire charge, listen for any adjustments in depth, repeat. He had no sense of the passage of time, nor did he allow his thoughts to settle on anything but the task at hand. The threat was real and their duty was clear: kill or be killed.

By the time they started their third pattern, the orange glow of the morning sun began to creep over the waters in the horizon. The splashes of the depth charges became clearer, as did the spewing fountains of water and mist that shot into the sky, which had steadily grew a lighter shade of blue. Despite the onslaught, there were no signs that they had struck the U-boat — no oil, debris, or larger explosion.[16] Jack remembers finally thinking to himself that the enemy had gotten away, which in the heat of the moment, he had not even considered until now. Afraid and charged by the reality of the situation, "you just focused on what you had to do and didn't really have time to think of anything else."

The final charge sent, he was ordered to cease fire. They had been at it for over an hour at this point, and had launched more than 30 depth charges. *Oakville* turned and combed the waters a bit — the ASDIC looking for a signal, but there was nothing bouncing against the sonar. Although he and his team were a little disappointed that they had not caught the U-boat, they were also relieved to be out of danger. They may not have destroyed the enemy, but the enemy had also failed to destroy them. Their retaliation was swift and fierce, and as Jack states: "if he was still in the area, I'm sure our attack sent him running."

The command came from the bridge for all stations to stand down. The morning sun was now in the sky, and from a cursory glance at the waters around them, it was clear they were alone, the convoy having continued on its way while *Oakville* had pursued the U-boat. Jack and the others secured their stations as the ship changed tack and steamed its way back towards the slow-moving convoy, waiting somewhere off in the distance.

"There was not much we could do," he explains. "We couldn't search around anymore; it was more important to get back to the convoy."

It was now time for some much-needed breakfast, which the crew was happy to have. Having been on edge, they had certainly worked up a healthy appetite. As he settled down with his food at the mess table, the conversation naturally turned to the recent encounter. Jack recalls his shipmates talking about how close the torpedo came to the ship, the damage a torpedo would have done had it struck the ship, whether or not they thought they managed to damage the U-boat, if they were near it at all, and if the enemy might try to attack again. But mostly, everyone was praising the quick thinking of both the OOW and the attentiveness of the starboard lookout.

"Everyone was excited all right," Jack explains. "They guy that saw the torpedo was given a lot of pats on the back and good boy praise."

"He saved the ship," I state, and Jack laughs.

"I think so. I hate to think what would have happened had he been dozing off or not paying attention. We might not be having this conversation, that's for sure!"

He laughs and then adds with some seriousness, "it was good that he didn't go all to pieces when he saw it."

In fact, the one thing that the crew took from this event was that despite the monotony of their watches, duties, and drills, they had to maintain situational awareness. If any of them had become slack in any of their duties, the close call certainly snapped them back to the reality that they were indeed at war.

"It certainly smartened me up," Jack admits. "I realized that I couldn't drop my guard, because the enemy would be waiting." After that point, "we knew they were out there. Watching and waiting." It certainly played on their nerves for a bit, and although the event had been eye-opening for many of the sailors aboard *Oakville*, including Jack, he was also proud that in the heat of battle he had done what he was trained to do — that they had all performed their duty.

Jack starts to chuckle again. This time it becomes infectious and I find myself laughing along with him.

"What are we laughing about?" I ask him.

"Oh, this story just reminded me about something I find funny," he answers. "You know, although I was a torpedoman by trade aboard *Oakville*, would you believe that I never once saw or touched a torpedo — not even the one that nearly struck the ship?"

"Maybe that wasn't such a bad thing," I tell him, and we share another laugh.

If there is one thing that Jack's story certainly announces about HMCS *Oakville* it was that the corvette was not only a tough and gritty fighting ship, but also a lucky one.[17]

LATTER YEARS

In October of the same year, shore radio stations located an enemy submarine south of Newfoundland. Once again, *Oakville* answered the call and accompanied a group with HMCS *Restigouche* to hunt it. This foray was a little different than the sneaky torpedo attack it had narrowly avoided a few months ago. Once in open waters, the weather quickly soured with force-nine winds and 40-foot seas. Sailors aboard the ships struggled to man their posts, and many of them had to stay the pangs and discomfort brought on by vicious seasickness. The weather continued to worsen the longer they were out, and despite their resolve, the order was given to return to port, forcing the hunt to be called before any of the ships reached the datum point.

It was the last bit of action *Oakville* would experience.

She continued with her escort duties without much excitement until April 2, 1945, when she was again refitted by Lunenburg Foundry and Engineering Ltd. There she remained until Germany surrendered in May and was not ready until June 4. As the distances in the Pacific campaign against Japan were far too great for corvettes, the decision was made to pay her off for disposal at Sydney on July 16, and she was towed to Sorel, Quebec to be laid up.

Her service in the RCN had ended.

Jack Russell was in Lunenburg, Nova Scotia when the ship went in for its refit. It was there that he discovered that the war was both over for him and the ship he'd called home for the past few years.

The engines were half torn down when they received the news that the ship, along with a bunch of other corvettes, were to head down to Sorel: "So, they put the engines back in and got them going good enough to work again for her trip down the St. Lawrence," he tells me. Jack would not join his ship for her last trip — he was going home for leave and, understandably, was quite excited about it. As far as everyone knew, it was going to be scrapped.

"Did you see it go?" I ask.

"Yeah, I did," he answers, and I catch a little something in his tone. Sadness perhaps, but I don't want to interject my own thoughts, so I follow with: "How did that make you feel?"

He pauses for a moment.

"Seeing it leave was tough but I wasn't sad," he admits. "It was, in our mind, the best one going, but it was one of those things that had to happen; I had no say in it."

HMCS *Oakville* in refit, Lunenburg, Nova Scotia, immediately after V.E. Day. (*Courtesy Edward Stewart.*)

Jack takes another moment, then adds that "the government said it had to be scrapped and that's where it went. It had seen its day probably." He tells me that he was happy to be going home to see his family and friends. He didn't think twice about the ship until later on. Then, back at home, he found himself thinking about his time aboard *Oakville*, of his friends and their time together. More and more, the ship occupied a deeper place in his heart.

"It was as good as any of them … maybe better," he says fondly. "I understand why the government did what it did, but I wish it could've been different."

FINAL BELL

Though *Oakville* was finished and decommissioned with the RCN, the corvette itself was still to see service beyond that of many of her sister ships. The Canadian government sold her to Venezuela, where she was recommissioned into their navy as the *Patria*. From October 17, 1945 to August 11, 1959, she would serve faithfully until being decommissioned for the final time.

Eventually, despite the efforts of some members of the historical society, the memory of this ship and its valiant crew faded from public consciousness, and the town forgot about the historical significance surrounding the christening and actions of its namesake warship. The town, whose mayor boasted that the christening and naming of a warship in its name would be a day "long remembered," forgot about its hero in only a few decades. The write-up of the "Men of Valour" poster would also disappear.

In fact, I distinctly recall seeing a picture of that very poster, minus the caption, when I was young — it was in my history textbook as an example of war propaganda.[18] The explanation was that the fantastical event depicted was *concocted* to rally support and recruitment. My teacher even agreed, stating how silly it would be to believe that men actually did such a "Hollywood"-like thing. Imagine my dismay when years later I discovered that it was

not fantasy at all, but something that actually happened — a proud moment, not only in Canadian history, but for the town in which I resided. It was an absolute disservice to the memory of that fine ship and her heroic crew.

Walk in Owen Sound and ask someone at random if they know who Billy Bishop was, and you will likely be told that he is Canada's most famous war ace, who won the Victoria Cross. Ask someone in downtown Oakville what HMCS *Oakville* is, or who Lawrence or Powell are, and they'll say "I don't know." At least, that's what happened when I tried doing just that.

And yet, there are sources that have always made note of *Oakville*'s famed conflict with U94. Even Lawrence published several accounts detailing the encounter. What was left out, however, was the whole story of the ship — her beginnings and christening. Ironically, the fame and attention surround-

Corvette *Oakville* after being sold to Venezuela and renamed *Patria*, 1949. (*Courtesy Oakville Historical Society.*)

ing *Oakville*'s fight against U94 overshadowed the historical significance and attachment it had with its namesake town. The moment *Oakville* transformed from an ordinary corvette, whose crew had been "adopted" by a small town, to a grand naval legend, it slipped away. The legend overshadowed the human aspect of the ship.

However, the spirit of *Oakville* and her crew would not be kept quiet indefinitely, and would once again resurface in none other than the very place where it first was born.

POST NOTE ON ITES

Ites and his crew were kept as prisoners of war by the US until May 1946. After returning home from the war he educated himself and went into dentistry. In 1956, with West Germany's accession into the North Atlantic Treaty Organization (NATO), a new German Navy was established — the *Bundesmarine* (Federal Navy). He joined the same year and served for two years as a commander of a destroyer, then assumed several staff positions. By the time he retired in 1977, he had obtained the rank of *konteradmiral* (rear-admiral). He died February 2, 1982.[19]

POST NOTE ON KING

Despite his tough manner and battle-hardened experience, King allowed a certain degree of informality aboard *Oakville*. According to Reg Adams:

> *Oakville* [in 1942–43] was not a pusser ship; by that I mean there was not too much navy routine. For instance, when entering or leaving harbour, all captain King demanded was that we wear our navy hats, whereas in some ships the crew would have to be in full uniform. After all, we were just a bunch of guys who had joined up to fight a war — and not to make a career out of it. I guess by now you realize we loved captain King.[20]

King would go on to command other ships, notably HMCS *Swansea* (four sunken U-boats to her name), and by the end of his naval career would be further decorated with a Legion of Merit (Legionnaire Grade), two Mention-in-Dispatches, and a bar to his Distinguished Service Cross. He retired with the rank of captain (navy) and died at the age of 77.

CHAPTER 5
The Long Revival

THE HARRY BARRETT LETTERS

In the 1980s, after a long slumber, HMCS *Oakville* began to emerge from the past. Mayor of Oakville Harry Barrett, himself a veteran of the Second World War, began gathering information regarding the corvette. On August 26, 1981, Acting Director of the Directorate of History, Norman Hillmer, wrote a letter to Air and Naval Attaché for the Venezuelan Embassy, Colonel Gilberto Estrella, requesting information about the Venezuelan ship *Patria*, formerly HMCS *Oakville*. His office had a letter, dated October 11, 1957, stating that the Venezuelan government was contemplating "making a hydrographic survey ship out of one of the four ex-Canadian corvettes in the Venezuelan navy."[1] He sought to discover if *Oakville* had anything to do with that, as well as what became of her after the ship was removed from their country's naval list in 1962. On January 10, 1982, he received a response from Colonel Estrella, though it did nothing more than confirm that after 1947 the ship had served in the first division of corvettes, and on August 11, 1959, was sent to the National Shipyard.

Barrett was not satisfied and began doing his own searching, during which he contacted the Venezuelan ambassador. He sent His Excellency Victor Delascio a letter requesting assistance. In the letter he detailed how *Oakville*, named "to honour our municipality"[2] was a "prominent" ship in the history of the RCN, and that much interest existed about the ship. He wished to know about her service in the Venezuelan navy and what happened to the ship after being removed from naval service. His keenness on the condition of the ship indicated the growing interest in the community. In reading his letter to the Venezuelan ambassador, it becomes apparent that Barrett had high hopes for *Oakville*. He states, "In the event that she is still afloat, we would possibly consider repatriating her to our municipality and treat her in a similar manner that the City of Toronto has treated the HMCS *Haida*."[3] Also, in the likely event of her disposal, "… any memorabilia that is available and could be forwarded to us would be most appreciated."[4]

On March 17, 1983, he dispatched a letter to the Minister of National Defence, Hon. Gilles Lamontagne, requesting assistance in gathering information on HMCS *Oakville*. Further, he was keenly interested in obtaining any memorabilia or artifacts from the ship for a town display — especially the ship's bell (which would have been the one donated by the town in 1941). Lamontagne's response in April was only slightly helpful. Aside from providing copies of the vessel's career history, the only relic known to the department of national defence was the ship's White Ensign, which had been presented to Branch No. 23 of the Royal Canadian Legion, Lunenburg, Nova Scotia by Lieutenant-Commander King.

In September, after having received no response from the Venezuelan Ambassador, he wrote to the Minister of Defence of Venezuela, Colonel J.I. Colmenares. His letter again mentioned the importance of the ship, the municipality's desire to repatriate the ship or acquire relics, and requested information on what happened to her after having entered the Venezuelan navy. He attached the letter forwarded by Lamontagne. In October, he received a response from the Venezuelan Air and Naval Attaché Office, which included a copy of a letter from the Venezuelan navy, indicating that they were currently searching to see if any parts of the ship could be obtained.

On March 21, 1984, Barrett dispatched another letter to Mr. Colmenares, indicating that he had yet to hear any further information and that he was "receiving frequent enquiries as to the progress of my enquiries to yourself concerning this vessel and the possible acquisition of artifacts and information."[5] In June, he wrote to Ken MacPherson of the Ontario Archives, having been informed that Mr. MacPherson had both photos and information regarding the corvette. His response in August came with information, a photo of the ship, and the opinion that HMCS *Oakville* had surely "... long since been scrapped or scuttled." He also noted that "... it would be a minor miracle should any artifact remain in existence."[6]

Barrett still persisted, contacting Colonel Sergio Galindez in 1985 with the same enquiry. Unfortunately, at the end of the day, news regarding the fate of *Oakville* was disappointing. The Venezuelan government indicated that no artifacts were available and that the ship had indeed been scrapped. HMCS *Oakville* was gone.

JOHN ALFORD'S PAINTING

In November 1983, Barrett received a letter from Manuge Galleries Limited, informing the town that John Alford had painted a series of oil paintings commemorating Canadian naval vessels, and that HMCS *Oakville* was one of those vessels. Alford, born in England, was a distinguished naval artist who had even been commissioned by the British armed forces. His 24-inch by 36-inch portrait of HMCS *Oakville* depicted both Lawrence and Powell aboard the injured U-boat, with the corvette's damaged bow nearby and the convoy in the background. The gallery wished to know whether the town or any local legion would be interested in purchasing the painting for $3,200. Barrett was indeed interested and Don Blenkhorne volunteered to view the portrait and negotiate a discounted price. The town purchased the large portrait in March 1984. Harry sent letters regarding the picture to John C. Blakelock and the Lieutenant Governor, The Honourable John Aird, an ex-naval officer. In May, he contacted the gallery regarding making copies of the picture for interested residents.

Although beautiful, the painting erroneously portrays the ship. Barrett had also mentioned the painting in his letter to MacPherson, who quickly noted that "... the artist was led astray by having worked from a 1945 photo of the ship."[7] Indeed, the painting depicts *Oakville* without the short fo'c'sle and instead shows the vessel as it was after being re-fitted in Galveston, Texas. However, despite this technical error, the portrait is a lovely depiction of an important event in Canadian naval history. Today it hangs prominently in the main foyer of the Oakville Town Hall.

THE CAIRN TO HMCS *OAKVILLE*

Oakville Legion Branch 114 was keen to ensure that HMCS *Oakville* received some manner of formal commemoration. A committee was created with the mandate of erecting a cairn in Tannery Park to honour the officers and men who served aboard the town's namesake warship. In 1988, the Oakville Legion had a notice published in *The Legion* magazine, requesting that former members of *Oakville* make contact with the legion for a reunion. A slew of letters from Fred L. Garner, Donald Mann, J.W. Ward, Alan R. Mitchell, and even Arthur Powell, who in his letter referred to himself simply as "... the Stoker Petty Officer from the HMCS *Oakville*,"[8] came back in response. The president of the branch, Robert C. Charlton, wrote to the editor of *The Star Shell* magazine for the Naval Officers Association of Canada (NOAC), requesting that a notice be published indicating that Branch 114, along with local Sea and Air Cadet units, the local historical society, and other commercial and business groups, were working to erect a cairn to HMCS *Oakville*, with a ceremony to tentatively take place Sunday, June 11, 1989 at 2:00 p.m.[9] Major John Brierley, CO 540 Squadron Royal Canadian Air Cadets (RCAC) and member of HMCS *Oakville* Cairn Committee, had also written a similar request, which had already been answered on February 24, 1989. Unfortunately, they had missed the deadline for their notice to be published in the NOAC magazine, but other possibilities, including the *Navy League* magazine, were presented as alternatives. In addition, they provided any information regarding past COs and some other crewmembers regarding whom they had information. The notice was sent to a slew of Toronto, Oakville, Burlington, and Hamilton-based radio stations, newspapers, and television networks to ensure adequate press.

In February, Major Brierley also wrote to the Mayor of Oakville, Anne Mulvale, requesting a parade permit for June 11 as well as permission for the cadets to fire blank cartridges from a pair of field guns. He also noted that the lieutenant-governor would be in attendance and formally invited the town's dignitaries. The cairn committee continued to meet regularly from March through to April and produced detailed minutes regarding the planning and preparation for the event.

There was some resistance to allowing the gun salute for the ceremony. A local councillor at the time opposed the idea of a 17-gun salute, stating it was a "male-dominated" tradition that did not promote peace. Ward 3 councillor Kathy Graham argued that

it was a way to show respect for the men who served their country and argued that banning the act would be taken offensively by veterans. In the end, town council approved the motion in an 11-2 vote, waiving the anti-noise bylaw, as well as the bylaw prohibiting the discharge of firearms, to allow the mark of respect. As predicted, angry letters to the editor, notably a lengthy one by Trevor Harness, were received by the local newspaper in response to the councillor's comments.[10]

The legion began writing letters inviting past members of *Oakville* to attend the ceremony. On June 7, 1989 the local newspaper announced: "Cairn will honour the HMCS *Oakville*," noting that the Lieutenant Governor, Lincoln Alexander, would personally unveil the commemorative cairn during a ceremony hosted by 540 squadron RCAC, Branch 114 of the Royal Canadian Legion, and the Burlington Branch of the Royal Canadian Naval Association. Lincoln Alexander served as the 24th lieutenant-governor of Ontario from 1985–1991. He had served in the Royal Canadian Air Force during the Second World War, was a graduate of Osgoode Hall Law School, and became Canada's first black Member of Parliament in 1968. Considering the corvette's history, having such a distinguished guest of honour was certainly fitting for *Oakville*.

On the day of the celebration, a parade formed just outside the Oakville Legion on Church Street at 1:00 p.m. It was a sunny day with few clouds, a slight breeze causing the flags to ripple in the wind. The sea cadet band led the procession, dressed in ceremonial whites and playing their instruments, followed by a colour party manned by naval veterans. Trailing closely behind was sea cadet "Ceremony of the Flags" division, and then a sea cadet guard of approximately 80 cadets with rifles and fixed bayonets. In their wake they towed a naval field gun, its silver metallic barrel glinting in the early afternoon sky. Behind them marched the guests of honour — veterans of HMCS *Oakville*, the division rather appropriately led by Arthur Powell. Spaced some 40 feet behind were members of the Oakville legion, a small division of women from the Women's Royal Naval Service[11] (WRNS) followed by yet another colour party, this time of air cadets, followed respectively by an air cadet band and squadron. It was a very large parade. From the Oakville legion, the parade headed south on Navy Street, turned right on Lakeshore Road, Left on Chisholm Street, and finally left on Walker Street to Tannery Park.

The procession arrived at Tannery Park at 1:45, where Captain D.M. Pyne CD made an introduction, indicating that the sea cadet's ceremony of the flag group were from all across Ontario. He warned the crowd that after the ceremony there would be a salute with the naval field gun and that people should protect their ears.

The lieutenant-governor arrived at 2:00 p.m. in full Canadian Forces Air Force uniform[12] and received the Vice Regal Salute. A Royal Canadian Sea Cadet band played "The Queen,"[13] followed by an inspection of a guard of honour. Present members of HMCS *Oakville* were introduced, including Arthur Powell, Merlin Smith, Bob Jaeger, John McKeown, Blake Morash, and Fred Garner. The cairn, draped with the White Ensign, was then unveiled by the lieutenant-governor, followed by the playing of "The Last Post" and "The Lament" by Mr. Bruce Taylor (of the Salvation Army) and Pipe Major Bill Robertson, respectively.

The Reveille was then sounded, followed by an address from Alexander, who spoke of the importance of never forgetting the sacrifice made by the crew of HMCS *Oakville*. Standing tall in his blue uniform, complete with medals and decorations, he addressed the assembled veterans, cadets, and guests with the ease and charisma of a seasoned orator, never once glancing at a sheet of paper. Fortunately, the legion documented the event on film and thus Alexander's inspiring words to the crowd and crew of HMCS *Oakville* have survived:

> … how delighted I am to be here this afternoon. Lest we forget, we shall not forget. This is truly a historic occasion. When I think that the HMCS *Oakville* was christened on the fifth of November 1941 and now I have the opportunity, and had the opportunity, unveiling a cairn to commemorate the officers and crew of the HMCS *Oakville*. You know I had a short stint in the Royal Ca-

Lieutenant-Governor Lincoln Alexander unveils the cairn dedicated to HMCS *Oakville*. (*Courtesy Edward Stewart.*)

nadian Air Force. And I guess these Navy types don't mind me saying that — they always want to remind me of which is the senior service and I always say "oh"?

He paused while the crowd, mostly naval veterans, laughed.

… But you know I am reminded of the many young people, who at that time, with me and others, served — whether it was on land, air, or sea — and the result of that service: some paid with their lives, others are here with us to enjoy this beautiful day, and I can only think that thank-God we had those young people who were prepared to serve their country. Let it be a lesson to all these young people, that there comes a time when you must put up! And that's a wonderful experience to have in order to say "I'm doing this for my country," and it's the result of what those people did, here we stand today, to enjoy freedom. Living in a country that is

the envy of many of the developing countries — all the developing countries and some developed countries. Truly a wonderful experience that we're living here today. I salute those who were involved with the HMCS *Oakville* and, ladies and gentlemen, what is so important today is here they are …

Alexander turned and gestured to the veterans of HMCS *Oakville*, who were seated behind him, Powell in the centre. The crowd applauded.

… though they're from all over, still looking splendid in their uniform, in their legion uniforms or their suits as the case may be, but coming here so that they can remind us of what happened back in 1942–1945 on that wonderful corvette! We have to face it — they're one of only three corvettes who sank a submarine. Gentlemen, it's very hard for me to put into words what must be said, but let me say the nation is indebted to people such as yourselves and those that weren't

Veterans of HMCS *Oakville*. Note: far left is Arthur Powell, wearing his Distinguished Service Medal. (*Courtesy Edward Stewart.*)

able to come back — lest we forget, we shall not forget! And I'm always interested in those words "lest we forget." Sometimes it seems to me that people forget what happened back in 1945, 42 to 45. Sometimes people don't want to remember. Sometimes people want to forget that veterans are still around. And some paid a tremendous price! Lest we forget, we shall not forget. I want to thank the legion, the president, and all those whom he represents, together with the cadets, air, navy, army, and the community at large for seeing to it that this day has come about. It's going to live long in the memory of all of us here — it's so picturesque, it's so colourful. We have the youth, surrounded by the seasoned veterans, those who have served, and those parents looking on at the youth, praising them. We must praise the enthusiasm of these young cadets; we must, we must tap their energies!

Again, the crowd clapped and the lieutenant-governor took a brief moment before carrying on.

.... We must believe in, we must believe in their dreams, we must help them to accomplish those dreams. Let me say I'm singly honoured to stand here as her Majesties representative, proud as punch! Proud indeed to represent our gracious Majesty on this particular day in order to extend to every one of you, and particularly the veterans, thank you for serving and for serving so well. To you, all the organizers, congratulations for a job well done.

And to all of you, may God continue to watch over and bless you. Thank you very much.

A speech by Lieutenant-Colonel J.M. Anderson, MC, CD gave a blessing and dedication, which was followed by a gun-salute by the sea cadets, and a ceremony of the flags display. The sea cadet band then played "O Canada" before the parade departed, marching back to the Oakville Legion and saluting the viceregal on Lakeshore Road. Over 100 people were reported to be in attendance, including 540 Squadron and Royal Canadian Sea Cadet Corps (RCSCC) *Patriot*, *Crescent*, *Iron Duke*, and *Ojibwa*.

The cairn honouring HMCS *Oakville* in Tannery Park has a fieldstone finish, adorned by a 18-inch by 24-inch bronze plaque reading:

> To Commemorate
> The Officers and Crew of
> HMCS OAKVILLE
> 1942–1945.
> They Served in Canada's
> Time of Need.

After the erection of the cairn, interest in HMCS *Oakville* began to dwindle again. The momentum begun by Harry Barrett to preserve the ship's history had culminated with this tribute to the ship. However, much of the ship's history had yet to be uncovered — much of its story, both local and abroad, did not accompany the monument. The local legion never created a display to the corvette, and the town did little more to preserve the local history of the ship. Even the cairn plaque provided little detail — no mention of its christening, nor its encounter with U94. Within a decade, memory of the ship would fade from the public's mind, until it would become just another ship that served in the Second World War. For that reason, when efforts were finally made to establish a Royal Canadian Sea Cadet Corps in Oakville 10 years later, much of the ship's history would have to be re-discovered.

The cairn dedicated to HMCS *Oakville*. (*Courtesy Edward Stewart.*)

Lieutenant-Governor Lincoln Alexander poses for a picture with veterans of HMCS *Oakville*. P. J. McKeown is kneeling, second from the left. (*Courtesy P.J. McKeown.*)

CHAPTER 6
Passing of the Torch – The Birth of RCSCC *Oakville* and the Canadian Naval Centennial Parade

THE CANADIAN CADET MOVEMENT

Cadets is a national organization whose aim is to develop leadership, engaged and active citizenship, and physical fitness in youth, while stimulating an interest in the sea, land, and air elements of the Canadian Armed Forces (CAF). It is open to youth from all levels of society from the ages of 12–19, and all training costs and uniform expenses are assumed by the Department of National Defence (DND). It is the largest federally sponsored youth program in the country and currently consists of approximately 56,000 Cadets located in over 1,000 units in cities and towns all across Canada.

Cadets are encouraged to become responsible members of their communities and to understand the necessity of civic engagement. They learn the importance of giving back to one's community, and that they have a duty to be involved in community programs and to help make the cities and towns they live in better places for all residents.

Cadets are organized into units that reflect the three elements of the CAF and participate in local, regional, and national activities. They are instructed by members of the Cadet Instructor Cadre* (CIC), who are fully commissioned reserve officers that have been specially trained to instruct, supervise, and motivate youth. Though the program is funded by DND and local units are operated by CAF personnel, the purpose of Cadets is not to provide a recruiting pool for the CAF. Rather, they learn how to become productive members of a team and how to instruct, time-manage, and plan and conduct activities — valuable skill sets that are often neglected for youth. Cadets are encouraged to seek and plan for personal success in all venues. Some join the military, while others seek civilian careers. Whatever pathway they choose, the Cadet program undoubtedly aids in providing skills to help ensure their continued success.

The Canadian Cadet organization is part of a larger collective known as the Canadian Cadet Movement (CCM), which consists of:

- cadets
- cadet instructors — both military and civilian
- league members — civilian organiza-

---

* As of 2009, designation was changed to Cadet Organizations Administrative and Training Service (COATS)

tions that provide financial support, as well as facilities and storage space for cadet corps and squadrons

- DND — which provides training equipment, uniforms, and qualified CAF instructors

These groups work together to create a positive and enriching learning environment. The vision statement of the CCM declares:

> We commit to develop in each and every Sea, Army and Air Cadet qualities of leadership and an aspiration to become a valued member of his or her community. We reinforce values necessary to prepare youth to meet the challenges of tomorrow and to embrace the multicultural dimensions of Canada. To this end, we offer dynamic training in a supportive and efficient environment where change is a positive and essential element. We further commit to attain this vision by living shared Canadian values, paying particular attention to: LOYALTY, PROFESSIONALISM, MUTUAL RESPECT, INTEGRITY.

OAKVILLE REVIVED

During the mid-1990s, the town of Oakville did not have a Sea Cadet corps. Royal Canadian Sea Cadet Corps (RCSCC) *Chaudiere*, a Milton-based Sea Cadet corps, established a "B Company" in Oakville to satisfy growing interest among locals in the program. I was a member of this Sea Cadet group for a year before leaving to join the Primary Reserves. As interest grew, talk of establishing a separate Sea Cadet corps in Oakville began. For the Town of Oakville, whose

name adorned one of Canada's most distinguished naval ships, the choice was clear.

THE TORCH BEARERS

The historical importance of a Cadet corps is often understated. A Sea Cadet corps serves as a living link to its region's nautical past. Often named after a real Canadian warship, its cadets wear the same ship's crest, cap tallies, and ship identification, and are not only taught about the ship's past but proudly represent it within their community. Cadets of RCSCC *Oakville* are not only proud to represent this esteemed ship but feel privileged to carry its name and memory within the community. When a cadet is presented with their corps badge, they understand the history and significance behind it, and the honour and responsibility associated with it.

Creating a Sea Cadet corps is not easy. It requires the formation of a local Navy League branch as well as community interest. Aside from the bureaucratic process, the greatest challenge for the founders of RCSCC *Oakville* was the ship's history — the foundational legacy of the corps. Naturally, they would be named after the ship, but what exactly was *Oakville*? Though they knew of the ship, and of its historical encounter with U94, little else of the ship's history — specifically its ties to the community — remained. Local naval historian Edward Stewart, branch president Elaine Nielsen, and member Linda Gignac began investigating. They began contacting museums and surviving crewmembers, and dug into news archives to find information.

On August 4, 1999, Howard Mozel of the local newspaper posted an article titled "Mystery deepens as sea cadet organizers delve into past of HMCS Oakville." In his article he notes that the attempt to establish a new Sea Cadets corps in Oakville had "... assumed the air of a detective story."[1] Discovering the ship's artifacts and locating missing crewmembers, a journey that Barrett had commenced years ago, had proved difficult. Gignac was a *Toronto Star* employee and used her connections to conduct research into the ship's history. The local historical society also had the ship's original clock, donated by the Marlatt family, and talks with the Venezuelan government continued again, with the hopes of acquiring a piece of the original ship. "Even to have part of it would be exciting," Gignac was quoted as saying. The most coveted artifact was the ship's bell. "There is a whole mystery angle to this," Gignac said, explaining that multiple stories regarding the fate of the bell had surfaced. Perhaps the most fruitful discovery Gignac made was images of *Oakville*'s badge. Unfortunately, as the images were black and white, the colour scheme remained a mystery. As well, two of the 30-inch by 36-inch crests that had adorned the ship's gun shields, as well as a third (which had hung in Oakville's council chamber) were missing, though their image clearly showed how the ship's crest was based on the town's own coat of arms. In fact, many of the crewmembers that replied to Gignac's enquiries did not believe that *Oakville* even had a crest, since it was never actually secured to the ship.

The article noted that DND had placed the operation of the corps under the command of Lieutenant (Navy) (Lt(N)) Steve Cooper, CO of RCSCC *Iron Duke* in Burlington, for the coming training year.

Mozel wrote a follow-up article on July 11, indicating that "the exciting effort now underway to establish the Royal Canadian Sea Cadet Corps Oakville will pay homage to local history as well as to the future."[2] Branch president Elaine Nielsen was quoted as saying: "As we go into the new millennium we are bringing the past with us in a positive way.… I think it should be very meaningful to a lot of people in Oakville."[3] Nielsen noted that the cadets, with their white tops bearing cap tallies with the ship's name, would "… soon become one of the visible symbols of our lakefront town."[4] The article further noted that the corps would not only be named after the town's famous warship but that its number (178) would also be the same. Plans for the corps formation were set for May 28, 2000, with a ceremony starting at the Oakville Curling Club. From that location, the corps would parade along Lakeshore Road to Navy Street, and then down to Lakeside Park to receive a gun salute from HMCS *York* and *Star* from the pier. Naval Cadet Bryan McIntyre stated that the "stand-up" would mirror the original christening ceremony as closely as possible.

On September 19, more answers emerged as the original gun shield crest of HMCS *Oakville* was displayed. Due to the quality of the protective metal and the failure to drill a bit to penetrate it, the shield had not been placed on the ship and had fallen into the possession of the Litchfield family. Maurice and Darryl Litchfield produced the relic, which confirmed the colours of the ship's crest. In addition, the article mentioned that 178 cap tallies had been made and that four would be auctioned at a later date for fundraising purposes. Plans had also changed for the corps start-up ceremony. It would now take place at St. Jude's Anglican Church in Oakville on November 6 at noon — a day after the original christening of *Oakville*. It would be the last Sea Cadet corps of the century to be created.[5]

Treasurer Gerry Lubanszky drafted a financial plan to secure both interim and long-term funding for the Oakville branch from the Ontario division of the Navy League of Canada. He proposed seeking from the division a loan of $25,000 (accompanied by an operating budget drawn by the corps CO). The proposal was presented by Nielsen and Lubanszky to the Divisional Executive Committee, which recommended that the corps seek a new line of credit as opposed to a loan, and that the account be utilized solely for the purchase of capital assets. In addition, for the interim, the committee provided a $3,000 line of credit to cover initial operating costs.

On September 15, 1999, officers, cadets, and parents of the new cadet corps were invited, along with members of the Oakville branch, to the first annual general meeting in the Normandy room of Royal Canadian Legion Branch 114. The first executive committee for the branch was elected — everything was now set for the corps' official commissioning.

SHIP'S BADGE

As already noted, HMCS *Oakville* did not initially have a ship's badge. Unlike modern-day warships, whose crests are designed and granted before their entering service, it would be well after her christening that *Oakville* would have one designed. Unfortunately, despite the good-natured intentions of the people of Oakville, the ship would never have a chance to display her crest.

In an article appearing in the *Toronto Daily Star* on March 31, 1943, the title read: "Gun Shields of Adopted Ship To Bear Oakville Town Crest."[6] At a council meeting in Oakville, Mayor Deans communicated that he had received a request from Lieutenant-Commander Clarence A. King, who at the time was still in command of *Oakville*, to arrange a placing of the gunshield crests aboard the ship.

Prior to this, the idea of having a ship's badge that bore the likeness of the crest of the Town of Oakville had been discussed as early as the ship's christening. However, it would be King who would propose the crest design, which was done at HMCS *Cornwallis* in early 1943. Dimensions of the gunshield would be "… five feet six inches high by six feet long."[7] In addition, there would be "… two crests, one for each side of the shield. Each crest will measure approximately 30 inches wide by 36 inches high."[8]

Mayor Deans announced to council and assembled press that they were "… proud of this opportunity of presenting our adopted ship with the town's crest,"[9] and that the crests would be a faithful representation of the town's own crest, right down to colour.

The image presented in the article is the same as the original picture, dated Instructional Division Gunnery Dept. HMCS *Cornwallis*, February 24, 1943 and with the initials J.F.E. The image was done in black and white, although the gunshield was made in colour. Within a lozenge-shaped frame, it depicts a white oak, with a small boat sporting 12 oars, and the word "AVANCE," the town's motto, on the bottom. Above the tree are three maple leaves, each with a sinister-facing beaver with a crown. At the top of the frame is the ship's nameplate with the naval crown.

However, after HMCS *Oakville*'s battle with U94, each member of the crew was given, as a gift from the town of Oakville, a wood plaque bearing the town's crest.

Wooden plaque given to all members of HMCS *Oakville* by the city of Oakville after the corvette's sinking of U94. The plaque was donated to Branch 32 by Comrade P.J. McKeown. (*Courtesy Edward Stewart.*)

Although the crest on the plaque bears the name "Oakville" and the diamond-shaped frame and naval crown, the image and colours of the plaque given to the crew of HMCS *Oakville* do not match the gunshield's image. Additionally, the crest of the town of Oakville — at least any image that could be found — does not seem to match the image found on this plaque, which is puzzling. To compare, the coat of arms for the town of Oakville, designed by Stanley Arculus, contains many elements that represent the community: the oak tree in the centre represent Colonel William Chisholm (1788–1842), whose nickname was the "White Oak," and the town's namesake tree. On either side of the tree are boar heads, which come from the Chisholm family coat of arms. Below the tree is a boat, a reference to the town's early ship-building role, and below that are the blue waters of Lake Ontario. The background of the crest is red. The plaque given to the sailors of HMCS *Oakville* was far from accurate in its depiction of a city skyline below a blue sky with a large tree in the centre (which does not seem to perfectly resemble an oak tree).

Darryl Litchfield, whose father is credited for saving *Oakville*'s gunshield, tells the story of how the badge was saved from being scrapped. He indicates that his father, Maurice, noticed the crest in his uncle's office and was told that it was one of three crests created for the corvette, two of which were for the ship and the other for the town. Originally, the idea was to install the crests during the ship's christening ceremony, however, "... because of the armouring on the forward gun turret only one crest could be installed due to time constraints."[10] Apparently, the one in the office was put in the care of Litchfield's great uncle to be installed on the ship if the opportunity were to ever present itself. Litchfield also provides clarity on some details of the gunsheild itself, in particular the image found on the three maple leaves above the tree. According to his account, the Chief of Police, David Kerr, was responsible for "the patterns required to cast the metal ... as he was a professional pattern maker by trade," and that the chief, "evidently added his own unique piece of history by adding three beavers to the upper portion of the plaque [using] buttons off his police tunic to obtain the impressions."[11] Litchfield notes that a naval officer, having noted the difference between the gunshield's image and physical manifestation, had come to the conclusion that the badge in their possession was likely "... a forgery, as the Navy would never allow any tampering of the official crests' plan."[12] Interestingly, after the war, Litchfield's great uncle tried to donate it to the local historical society, "... but they didn't want it because of the painful memories of the War and they didn't seem to appreciate any historical significance that it may have held."[13] Additionally, the Town also refused the badge as they already were in possession of one (oddly, their version of the crest has not survived) and thus Litchfield's father took possession of it and, decades later, when the Oakville Navy League besought the public for artifacts related to the ship, he presented the crest.

HMCS *Oakville* gunshield. (*Courtesy Oakville Museum.*)

When it came time to approve a crest for the new Sea Cadet corps, Gignac contacted the Directorate of History and Heritage at National Defence Headquarters in Ottawa and sent them an image of the gunshield. Canadian Forces Heritage Officer, Major P.E. Lansey, replied that they had "no record of the 'unofficial' badge"[14] she provided. In his letter he noted that "early unofficial badges were of any shape as thought out by their designers, but when the badges were put on an official footing in 1948 the shape of the frames were categorized."[15] He further noted that "the Canadian Navy uses the 'Standard Design' which is round," and explained that the "... Royal Navy use a variety of badge frames and in their service the diamond shaped frame denotes auxiliary vessels."[16] Lastly, he stressed that "it is unlikely that the designers of the *Oakville* badge followed correct heraldic practices when it came to colours," and as such, he was not able to "... guess at the types or significance of the colours used."[17] Hence, it was only when the Litchfield family generously produced the original gunshield that colours of the original crest became apparent. Major Lansey did conclude that the "… three maple leaves in the central device gives a Canadian theme" and that "the inclusion of an oak tree is self evident."[18] With the colour of the crest revealed, and the response from the Directorate of History and Heritage acquired, the Navy League of Oakville moved forward with designing a badge for RCSCC *Oakville*.

When authority is granted for a Sea Cadet badge to be worn on a Canadian Forces Cadet uniform it becomes a CAF badge, subject to the same design criteria as the regular force. As such, it became evident that *Oakville*'s crest would have to meet the navy's criteria. Interestingly, as the gunshield was still unofficial, HMCS *Oakville*, in effect, never had an official crest. As such, creating a badge for the Oakville Sea Cadets would, as a result, create the first official badge for the corps' namesake corvette.

In 1983, the CAF Inspector of Badges, whose role it is to establish and maintain all CAF badge designs, conferred upon the Navy League of Canada the responsibility of designing, approving, and maintaining RCSCC badges. Similarly, the Navy League established its own inspector of badges in 1995, and in 1999 the position was held by retired Commander W.A. West. It was to West that the gunshield and colour scheme were sent for the purpose of drafting a badge for RCSCC *Oakville*.

With such attention and scrutiny paid to the details of the badge of HMCS *Oakville* and the Sea Cadet badge modelled after it, the question arises: Why do ships even have badges? — where does this practice come from? Originally, it was common for all naval ships to a have a figurehead at the stem, a visual representation of the ship's spirit or character (it also could represent the ship's name, where applicable). As centuries passed, technological advances in shipbuilding saw the replacement of wooden hulls with iron and steel, and as such, figureheads became impractical. However, it did become customary to mount the figurehead of an old ship onto the quarterdeck of its predecessor. As stated in the guide to Naval Heraldry for Royal Canadian Sea Cadet Corps and Navy League of Canada Cadet Corps, newer ves-

sels were often designed with bow embellishments: "… to decorate the straight stems of iron warships [in the form of] gilded scrollwork, often with a heraldic device representing the ship's name, fitted high up on the ship's stem and flowing back on both sides of the bow above the hawse pipes."[19]

From this would develop the modern form of ship badges. As the design of ships became more practical, heraldic designs were "… often displayed as a bronze or brass casting on the quarterdeck or on the tampions of the ship's guns."[20] However, any form of standardization would not occur until after the First World War, when the College of Arms took responsibility for the design of ship's badges. They decided that all badges must be placed in a frame of rope, "… ensigned by a "naval crown" and with the nameplate superimposed on the upper portion of the badge just below the crown."[21] The shape of the badge's rope frame denoted the type of ship:

- Circular: capital ships
- Pentagonal: cursiers
- Shield-shaped: destroyers and submarines
- Lozenge-shaped: carriers and auxiliary vessels[22]

During the First and Second World War, the RCN followed suit when it came to creating badges for its own ships, and by 1948 all RCN ships, regardless of their class, would be assigned badges with circular frames.[23]

Oakville's badge would be made circular. On August 31, 1999, West contacted the Oakville Navy League with a badge design for the corps.

The new design featured, in West's words, "Gules (red) a white oak proper, standing on a vert (green) mount, and charged on the trunka bireme (double-decked oared boat) with 12 oars argent (white)."[24] In his letter to the Oakville Navy League, he explained that he had "… used the shape of the original HMCS *Oakville* tree and have made the foliage shape with the actual shape of the oak leaf,"[25] which he appropriated from another RN ship's badge

RCSCC *Oakville*'s badge. (*Courtesy RCSCC* Oakville.)

that also featured an oak tree. The white oak, naturally, symbolized the tree that populates the town of Oakville, while the boat symbolized the "white oak" schooner that was built in Oakville harbour and sailed out to sea on Dominion Day, 1867. Like its namesake town, the motto for the corps remained "Avance."

Both HMCS and RCSCC *Oakville* now had an official badge.

OAKVILLE'S SECOND COMMISSIONING

On Saturday, November 6, RCSCC *Oakville* was officially launched, 58 years after its namesake ship was commissioned in 1941. Acting as reviewing officer was Captain (Navy) (Capt(N)) John A. Keenliside CD, chief of staff of the Canadian Forces College in Toronto. The parade began at 11:00 a.m. with 37 Oakville Sea Cadets and officers marching from Royal Canadian Legion branch 114 to the town square on Lakeshore Road.

RCSCC *Chaudiere* provided an honour guard. They were then inspected by Keenliside, who in his address to the corps said: "For those of us getting up in years we tend to look to the past, and it's up to you to look to the future."[26]

SLt A. Moore, followed by Lt(N) S. Weatherhead, leads cadets from RCSCC *Chaudiere* and *Oakville* to Oakville town square. (*Courtesy Edward Stewart.*)

Capt(N) Keenliside CD, reviewing officer for RCSCC *Oakville*'s start-up. (*Courtesy Edward Stewart.*)

In attendance were Gary Wintermute, president of the Ontario Division of the Navy League of Canada, Oakville MP Bonnie Brown, and Mayor Ann Mulvale. Just as with the original ship's christening, both federal and local politicians were present. In addition, several of the guests had also been present during the original ship's christening ceremony. From Town Square, RCSCC *Oakville* marched south on George Street and along William Street to St. Jude's Anglican Church, where the formal ceremony and blessings began at noon. Officiating were the Rev. Canon Bill Thomas, Chaplain of UNTD, Canon Pastor of Christ Church Cathedral in Hamilton, and Archdeacon William Hewitt of St. Jude's. Following the ceremony, a reception was held in Victoria Hall, with several of the ship's artifacts on display.

HMCS *Oakville*'s former executive officer Kenneth Culley wrote back to Linda Gignac from his home near Abercorn in the eastern townships south of Montreal, on September 11, 2000. In his letter he notes how happy he was to hear that there was growing interest in the history of his old ship:

RCSCC *Oakville* Flag Party. (*Courtesy Edward Stewart.*)

Inaugural officers, civilian volunteers, and cadets of RCSCC *Oakville*. (*Courtesy Edward Stewart.*)

Believe me, I find it most impressive especially in these days where pride in our armed forces seem somewhat old fashioned. And I am particularly pleased that someone from Oakville has not forgotten the ship and those who sailed in her. But what is more — that young Oakvillians (pardon me) are being given the opportunity of belonging to a most worthwhile organization which should help them develop skills and a sense of purpose and service.[27]

Strong bonds between HMCS *Oakville* and the Sea Cadet corps that would bare here name were being forged and, as evident from Culley's letter, the nod of approval had certainly been given to the new "torch bearers."

THE FINAL LINK

In February, the last link between RCSCC *Oakville* and her namesake ship was forged when Able Seaman Joseph Smyth, who had served aboard the corvette during 1943–1945, inspected the corps. Smyth had been a radar operator aboard *Oakville*, and though he had joined the ship after the historical battle, he did have experiences to speak of. He told the cadets: "I signed up for naval duty when the war was on because the advertisements said it was the only way to guarantee freedom, and I wanted my family and all families to be free."[28] Although he did not encounter any U-boats during his service, he did relate a tale when the ship had lost its steering and had floundered about the mid-Atlantic for 14 days. Food was growing scarce, so the captain ordered two depth charges dropped, whose explosion "… brought up enough fish to feed us until

105

we could make our way back to the port in Halifax."[29] He applauded the sea cadet program, and recalling gender restrictions during the war, he praised the fact that women were able to be Sea Cadets. "Women are a great asset to the navy," he said, "anyone can see that they're equal to, or better than the males."[30] He summarized his naval service, stating that he had entered a boy but had returned home a man — a significant statement, as all sea cadets leave the program having developed significant leadership, organizational, and interpersonal skills that enable them to contribute in their respective communities as engaged and active citizens.

THE NAVAL CROWN INAUGURAL BALL

The Oakville Navy League decided to plan an event in the wake of the new Sea Cadet corps' formation — a "grand scheme" as Ed Stewart relates it. The idea was to run a formal dinner and dance, not only to garner publicity and elevate the status of the new corps, but as a celebration of all those who served aboard the town's famed corvette. The event, which they called "The Naval Crown Inaugural Ball" was to be, as the name suggests, the first in an annual event that would bring together people in the community and celebrate its past and present naval ties. The event was set for April 28, 2001, not much more than a year after the formation of RCSCC *Oakville*. As advertised in the *Oakville Beaver*, it would be a black-tie event held at the St. Volodymyr Cultural Centre Grand Rotunda Reception in Oakville, complete with dancing to the Starlight Orchestra. Tickets for the event were being sold for $75 per person, or $600 per table of eight, the proceeds going to assist the league in finding a building[31] for the new Sea Cadet corps.

Oakville Navy League President Linda Gignac wrote letters to veterans of HMCS *Oakville*, inviting them as guests of honour to the event. She made note that there had never been a reunion for those who served aboard HMCS *Oakville*. Although some were able to attend the erection of the stone cairn at Tan-

nery Park in 1989, there had never been an initiative to re-establish ties for these veterans. The naval ball would be a chance to rectify that error and celebrate the memory of both the ship and its crew.

In the letter, she asked each veteran if they could send any information or pictures regarding their service aboard HMCS *Oakville* and encouraged the donation of any items. She even made mention that the league was hoping to make a book. She also included a cap tally of RCSCC *Oakville*, a cloth ship's crest, and a complimentary ticket. She indicated that the event location had a separate fireplace room available for them to relax in and mingle with their old shipmates.

As Ed Stewart explained, the event would feature speeches, including one from the mayor of Oakville, and was even set to have a large ice sculpture in the centre of the dance hall — a large sail, which was the former logo of the Navy League of Canada. However, despite its grand design, the event never did happen — it all amounted to what Ed called "a dull thud." The event simply never gained enough momentum, mainly due to the fact that the majority of responses returned to the Oakville Navy League sadly gave regrets, most noting poor health and age.

So why even make note of this failed event? Although only a few *Oakville* veterans were able to attend the event, Linda did receive a slew of responses. It is those responses, and their ties to HMCS *Oakville*, that deserve to be addressed.

One such response was sent from a "Doug MacLean," the same Douglas MacLean who was an ordinary seaman aboard *Oakville* during her encounter with U94. Writing from Calgary, Alberta, he reveals:

> At the time of the battle I was an ordinary seaman and my action station was operating the Oerlikon gun. Along with the captain and several other crew members that received decorations I was mentioned in dispatches. I later received my commission and when the war ended I held [the rank] of Lieutenant RCNVR[32]

This small White Ensign, being held by (*Left to Right*) Lt(N) Bryan McIntyre CD and Lt(N) Sean Livingston CD, belonged to Lieutenant-Commander Harold Lawrence and was donated by his wife to the new bearers of the ship's name. It was something he brought back from his time at sea and is dated March 1964. Although it didn't fly from any halyard on *Oakville* it certainly was a cherished keepsake from one of its most distinguished members. (*Courtesy Henry Lach.*)

Clearly MacLean showed promise as a leader and, as his letter reveals, moved from "before the mast"[33] to become an officer.

Chief Petty Officer and Chief Engine Room Artificer[34] Allan Mole, who served aboard *Oakville* from June 1943 to November 1944, wrote from Qualicum Beach, British Columbia that he had "... good memories of the ship and crew."[35] He goes on to say:

> I will not be able to attend the occasion but would like to pass on greetings to those members who might attend. The crew was predominantly from Eastern Canada with only 3 or 4 of us from the West Coast. I have not seen or been in contact with any member for almost 50 years and have often wondered how many are still about. My regards to those remaining members and wishes for your success with your affair.[36]

On March 8, 2001, Culley also wrote back, thankful for the invitation, but indicating that he and his wife "... would love to attend but must decline as we are no longer 'up' to such events."[37] Along with his well wishes, Culley revealed more about his career after *Oakville*:

The year I spent as Number One of HMCS *Oakville* have many memories. Before *Oakville* I had been overseas on course to the Royal Navy and after *Oakville*, I was Number One of another corvette — *Drumheller* — part of C2 group in mid-ocean Atlantic convoy duty. Then came a command course and back to C2 in command of yet another corvette — the *Morden*. When the war ended I was CO of *Long Branch* — a very modern corvette.[38]

He makes a postscript explaining that he made note of his commands in case "... some old shipmates may remember me."[39]

Gignac even received a reply from Alma Lawrence, Hal Lawrence's widow. Writing from Victoria, British Columbia, her letter dated May 10, 2000, she thanked Gignac for the corps crest and cap tally, noting, "We will treasure the cap tally and the handsome badge. My two eldest sons in particular as they were members of the Sea Cadets in Ottawa."[40] She also noted "... I do very little travelling these days but appreciated the invitation."[41] However, the most rewarding thing was she also included with her a letter an artifact — a small White Ensign that had belonged to her husband. Closing her letter, she indicated that it would be of "... more significance to the corps than at home," adding that "Lt-Commander Lawrence would have been very proud of your Sea Cadets and all the efforts you put in setting it up."[42]

Although the Naval Crown Inaugural Ball failed to reunite old shipmates, it was successful in acquiring some of the crew's experiences and in the gracious donation of an important relic.[43]

POST NOTE ON LIEUTENANT-COMMANDER KENNETH "KEN" CULLEY

On May 16, 2002, *Oakville*'s former executive officer died at the age of 89. He was the most senior member of the ship to have made efforts to communicate with the newly-founded Sea Cadet corps, and despite his health preventing him from attending both the corps stand-up and naval ball, he wrote more letters trying to assist the Oakville Navy League in answering questions about the famed corvette's past than any other veteran of the ship. For that reason, I find it fitting at this point to speak of his life both before and after HMCS *Oakville*.

Kenneth Lawrence Benjamin Culley was born in Newcastle upon Tyne, in Northeast England, on September 13, 1912. He grew up in London, where his first job was with the Bank of Montreal. In 1937 he moved to Canada and met his future wife, Ruth, who he married in July of 1940. Answering the call to king and country, Culley first tried to join the Royal Canadian Air Force but was unsuccessful in pilot school and thus joined the navy. He used his signing bonus to buy an engagement ring for Ruth. After the wedding he was shipped overseas for training. As noted in his obituary, posted in the *National Post* on May 16, 2002: "Later in life, he remembered arriving in Scotland on May 10, 1941, the same day Hitler's deputy, Rudolph Hess, crash-landed his plane in Scotland on a botched mission to end the war."

He made it back to Canada in time to be assigned to the newly built corvette *Oakville*.

When aboard HMCS *Drumheller*, Culley added yet another U-boat sinking to his war experience. U753 was attacked and sunk in the North Atlantic by depth charges from both *Drumheller* and the British Frigate HMS *Lagan*. Of the 31 U-boats to be sunk by the RCN* during the war — half of them with the advent of new technology and air support in the preceding two years — Culley had two successful engagements under his belt. By the end of the war he would have commanded two corvettes, HMCS *Morden* and HMCS *Long Branch*.

After the war, he returned home to Montreal and took up his old job with the bank. He also enjoyed theatre and radio, and "... once played Kent in *King Lear* when a 20-something Christopher Plummer took the lead role."[44] He was also involved in dramatic radio shows at the CBC. In the 1950s he did an advertisement

---

* Or that the RCN shared in sinking.

for Canada Savings Bonds, which was filmed "… live, and throughout the commercial, a fly was perched on his nose and he could not brush it away," and in 1967 he rather fittingly "… played an English sea captain in a French language television epic, *d'Iberville*."[45]

For over 50 years, he and his wife lived on an old farm they purchased south of Montreal. They had four sons.

OAKVILLE'S BELL – AN ONGOING MYSTERY

On November 27, 1941, the *Toronto Daily Star* announced: "Bell on Cairn Won't Ring Till War Ends or Ship Sunk." The article was in relation to the original ship's bell of HMCS *Oakville*. It announced the creation of a stone cairn (not to be mistaken by the one erected decades later in Tannery Park with Lincoln Alexander) that would be erected in a "public park" somewhere in Oakville; the location was not disclosed, as it likely was not yet confirmed. Above the cairn, the bell would be displayed. In a touching symbol of solidarity with the ship, the town pledged: "Its clapper will be sealed and there it will remain — a silent ship's bell until cessation of hostilities or until the ship is sunk."[46]

A sailor aboard HMCS *Oakville* ringing the ship's bell. (*Courtesy Edward Stewart.*)

How *Oakville*'s bell ended up not heading out to sea with the ship is explored in the article, which admits it being a "strange story." Construction crews originally fastened the bell onto the ship in its correct place on the bridge when it was being built in Port Arthur. From Lake Superior to the waters of Lakeside Park along Lake Ontario, the bell would see its only time of service — it would never make it to Montreal for the ship's commissioning into the RCN. As the article reveals:

> When the corvette sailed proudly into the port of Oakville, the vessel and its crew were adopted by the citizens. Not only did they give their name to the corvette but supplied every man aboard with sweaters and other wearing apparel, placed aboard a ship's library of 300 books and provided four radios for the officers and crew. They also expropriated the ship's bell.[47]

The identity of the men who removed the bell — who took pains to unfasten it from the bolts that secured it to the bridge — remain unknown, but in its place they left another bell, the one given to ship by the people of Oakville. The replacement was one that "shrieked of history with its every toll," having been salvaged from a ship that had sunk at Buzzard's Bay,[48] Massachusetts, and laid at the bottom for more than 50 years.

Clearly it was always the intention of the town and corvette committee to replace the bell and keep a living piece of the ship at home in Oakville. The new bell was given a gray coat of paint to match the original and to meet the strict and sensible guidelines put in place by the RCN: "[the bell] will be given its own coating of the gray paint of war that is unstintingly spread over these wartime fighting vessels of Canada."[49] The idea, as with all camouflage, was to help the ship blend in to its surroundings and make it less visible to the naked eye, which, at the time, was still the primary means of locating and identifying a ship at sea. Any shine or reflection from the sun's rays was to be avoided since it could betray their presence — much like a light at night — to the enemy:

> Even the bold brass letters that form the name of the corvette on either side of the sleek, gray vessel will be blotted out with gray paint or covered by a dark tarpaulin, so that when the vessel, soon to go into active service with the Canadian navy, sails into the Atlantic ocean she will be nameless and all but invisible at any distance.[50]

Permission from Naval Affairs had to be given for the handing over of the bell, which was generously granted by same dignitaries in attendance during *Oakville*'s christening, Nelles and Macdonald, but it did not occur until after the ship had already left Lake Ontario. The original bell, as it turns out, had remained on the ship and had to be sent "by express, with a tag attached giving Oakville its destination."[51]

And arrive it did.

The article makes note of a sobering point — as the town was clear in its idea to have the bell displayed, its clapper to remain silent until either *Oakville*'s triumphant return or loss to the enemy, the officers and sailors aboard the ship were very much aware that the "… ship's sinking," was "…something that may or may not be in the cards."[52]

If not for the actions of Acting Stoker Petty Officer David Wilson during *Oakville*'s battle with U94, the ship may have very well sunk from the wounds she received after ramming the U-boat. The bell was close to being rung to sound her loss at sea.

HMCS *Oakville*'s first captain weighed in with his own thoughts: "The clapper will be sealed until the cessation of hostilities, or, if the ship goes down, it will be tolled. If at the end of the war, the *Oakville* is still afloat, the bell will toll again."[53]

Whatever happened to the bell after that becomes sort of a mystery, one that has many stories. Apparently the bell used to be housed at the old Trafalgar Memorial, which was housed on the southeast side of

The plaque that accompanied HMCS *Oakville*'s bell. (*Courtesy Carolyn Cross.*)

the intersection of Trafalgar and Dundas Roads. Officially, the bell, along with a plaque, was donated to the Oakville Museum in 1954.

For some reason the museum's records indicate that it was catalogued as a "farm bell," donated by a Mr. Reginald Smith. The records indicate that the bell (but not the plaque) was transferred to the Oakville Historical Society for the Thomas House when the Museum and Historical Society became two separate entities. After that, the story largely becomes hearsay and speculation, which I wish to avoid. Suffice it to say that sometime after, the bell vanished. Decades later, Ed Stewart made attempts to track down the bell and the Oakville Sea Cadets made a plea for its return in the local newspaper.

Whenever a shipwreck is salvaged, the bell seems to be the key item, the one thing people wish to obtain. Perhaps it's because the bell of a ship is very much its soul. It is my belief (and that of many others) that the soul of *Oakville* is still out there, somewhere in Halton. Hopefully *Oakville*'s bell will one day turn up, so that the people of Oakville can ring it in memory of those men who served aboard her.

MUSEUM DISPLAYS AND CANADIAN NAVAL CENTENNIAL CELEBRATIONS

Prior to 2010, the Oakville Museum, coordinating with local naval historian Edward Stewart, held two museum exhibits on *Oakville*. The second of these, which opened Friday, May 12, 2006, had record attendance. As Ed Stewart recalls, "It was the first time in the museum's history that there was a line-up outside the building to see an exhibit." I gave a speech, along with Ed, on the opening night and walked patrons through the exhibit. Communal interest in the history of HMCS *Oakville* was being rekindled.

In early 2010 a committee was established — much like the corvette committee in 1941 — to help plan the Oakville Naval Centennial celebrations. Naturally, the focus would be on *Oakville*. The Canadian Navy had a plan to present plaques of ships in their

namesake town, and early in 2009 they contacted Ed to begin the process. Since our presentations in the museum (additionally, I made several school presentations in Oakville High Schools), interest had grown and the Oakville Museum was keen to highlight and honour this special part of the town's history. Curator of Collections, Carolyn Cross, formed a committee of various key community partners:

- Lt(N) Glenn Woolfrey MMM, CD, Representative — HMCS *Star*;
- Carolyn Cross, Curator of Collections — Oakville Museum;
- Susan Semeczko, Curatorial Assistant — Oakville Museum;
- Nigel Spink, Rear Commander — TOWARF;
- Ed Stewart, Naval Historian;
- Lt(N) Sean Livingston CD, Representative and Historian — RCSCC *Oakville*;
- Rod Adam, Landscape and Marine Artist;
- Rick Richarz CD, President — Branch 486 Legion;
- Mike Vencel, Parade Commander — Branch 486 Legion;
- Paul Visser, Chief of Staff — Town of Oakville.

The committee decided on utilizing a parade, which would follow as closely as possible the original parade route of the 1941 christening ceremony. There would also be the presentation by the navy of a plaque to the Town of Oakville, a tree planted with a plaque in memory of *Oakville*, and a large-scale museum exhibit (including a simulated radio room). I was to give an opening speech for the exhibit.

Both Carolyn Cross and Susan Semeczko were keen on the importance of creating a meaningful exhibit as part of the 2010 Canadian Naval Centennial. They decided on the name, *A Nod to the Navy: Oakville at Sea*, and began the work with the community to prep the event. As Carolyn later recounted:

Working with [community] partners to tell aspects of our town's history is always the most interesting part of preparing for an exhibit. It is the people's stories that add flavour to our past. History is not only about dates and events. Speaking with our residents, hearing their reminiscences of the November 5, 1941 parade, learning about artifacts held within their personal collections and having the privilege of viewing their personal photographs from the historic event brought the story to life for us.

Ed, who over the years collected and archived many photos of *Oakville*, provided the museum with most of its visuals, while my previous work was heavily drawn upon.

Carolyn Cross contacted Lieutenant (Navy) Glenn Woolfrey MMM, CD, having known him for several years, in order to ascertain what the navy had planned for the celebration. They began to brainstorm ideas and draft a list of community groups and people to contact and include in the committee. The committee (listed above) met at the Oakville Museum and, under the leadership of Lt(N) Woolfrey, created "… a single vision for the event, and worked tirelessly to organize the programme and events that took place on June 19, 2010."[54]

On the morning of June 19, 2010, the Town of Oakville paid tribute to the memory of HMCS *Oakville*. A parade formed on Navy Street, south of Trafalgar Road, which included the following participants:

- Members of HMCS *Star*'s company
- RCSCC *Oakville*
- Town of Oakville Water Air Rescue Force (TOWARF), Canadian Coast Guard Auxiliary
- Halton Regional Police Service Pipes and Drums
- Burloak Naval Veteran's Colour Party
- Veterans of both Oakville and Bronte Legions

- Scouts Canada youth and leader representatives

Most notably, joining the parade would be none other than Jack Russell and Joseph Smyth, both veterans of HMCS *Oakville*. Dignitaries for the event would be MPP of Oakville Kevin Flynn, Regional Chair Gary Carr, Mayor of Oakville Rob Burton, and TOWARF founder Fred Oliver.

By 9:45 in the morning the parade was ready. At 10:00 a.m. it would march south on Navy Street towards the Gazebo on Lakeside Park, across from Erchless Estate — the same location as in 1941.

Once mustered, the parade was turned over to the MC, Lt(N) Glenn Woolfrey. "O Canada" was sung by Heather and Lauren Woolfrey and Harrison Sutherland, followed by some opening remarks by Lt(N) Woolfrey.

Jack Russell and Joseph Smyth then unveiled the navy's plaque of HMCS *Oakville*, to be displayed in the Oakville Town Hall.

Remarks were made by the Mayor, Rob Burton, Regional Chair Gary Carr, and Oakville MPP Kevin Flynn. At 10:30 the parade moved to the tree dedication area, where the mayor made the presentation of both a horsechestnut tree and brass plaque. The Museum had arranged for a fly-past to emulate the 1941 event, but due to mechanical issues the aircraft was grounded.

Following the tree dedication, the crowd proceeded to the Museum for the formal opening of the exhibit by the mayor at 11:00 a.m., followed by my speech on *Oakville*.

It was undoubtedly the most popular exhibit in the museum's recent history. Carolyn Cross recalls her feelings that day:

> The day was memorable for me personally as it was about connecting people to one another. After the HMCS *Oakville* presentation, I remember talking with Christena Cook, a resident who was present at the 1941

Halton Regional Police Service Pipes and Drums. (*Courtesy Trish Feil.*)

Oakville Sea Cadets, led by Lt(N) Sean Livingston CD and Lieutenant Bryan McIntyre, and TOWARF. (*Courtesy Trish Feil.*)

parade. It was amazing listening to Christena openly share her memories of that day in 1941. It allowed me to gain a better understanding of how the war impacted our community. It also gave me a true appreciation of how our residents came together that day.

Although the exhibit was only scheduled to run until the end of July, it was extended to the fall due to popular demand. Carolyn Cross's reflection on that event nicely summarizes the importance, not only of HMCS *Oakville*, but also of keeping alive important elements of a community's past:

I believe that the coming together of the various community groups to plan and create a single vision for the event on June 19th … helped in preserving and celebrating Oakville's Naval heritage. Ultimately, leading the Town to gain a richer understanding of its past. The event made members of our community proud and in turn, instilled a sense of honour and respect for Oakville's Naval heritage.

Lt(N) Glenn Woolfrey MMM, CD, addresses crowd. To his left, Regional Chair Gary Carr, Oakville MPP Kevin Flynn, Jack Russell, and Joseph Smyth. RCSCC *Oakville* cadet PO1 Law is standing left of the plaque. (*Courtesy Trish Feil.*)

(*Left to Right*): Mayor Rob Burton; Jack Russell; Joseph Smyth; Lt(N) Woolfrey MMM, CD. (*Courtesy Trish Feil.*)

Plaque at base of tree. (*Courtesy Sean E. Livingston.*)

Model of HMCS *Oakville*, donated to the Oakville Historical Society by LCol G.T.J. (Jack) Barrett CD and Bdr. B.H. (Harry) Barrett RCA, generously loaned for the 2010 exhibit. (*Courtesy Trish Feil.*)

Communications room and RCNVR officer's overcoat, generously loaned by Lt(N) Woolfrey MMM, CD. (*Courtesy Sean E. Livingston.*)

Artifacts from Oakville, including the ship's chronometer, generously loaned by the Oakville Historical Society (as shown in Chapter 2), and simulated ship sounds. (*Courtesy Sean E. Livingston.*)

(*Left to Right*): Lt(N) Woolfrey MMM, CD; Christena Cook (resident present for 1941 parade); Jack Russell; Carolyn Cross; Susan Semeczko; and Lt(N) Livingston CD. (*Courtesy Trish Feil.*)

(*Left*)Museum exhibit, south wall. (*Courtesy Oakville Museum.*)

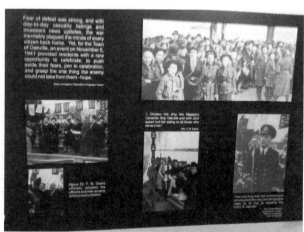

Another sample of the exhibit recounting *Oakville*'s christening. (*Courtesy Oakville Museum.*)

Exhibit with Powell and Lawrence featured in New York (far right). (*Courtesy Oakville Museum.*)

Jolene Schmidt, an art teacher from T.A. Blakelock, worked with her students to create commemorative stamps of Canadian warships and a group painting of HMCS *Oakville* (above) for the Oakville Museum exhibit. (*Courtesy Oakville Museum.*)

Quote from *Oakville's Forgotten Fame*. (*Courtesy Trish Feil.*)

Fear of defeat was strong, and with day-to-day casualty listings and incessant news updates, the war inevitably plagued the minds of every citizen back home. Yet, for the Town of Oakville, an event on November 5, 1941 provided residents with a rare opportunity to celebrate; to push aside their fears, join in celebration, and grasp the one thing the enemy could not take from them - hope.

-Sean Livingston,"*Oakville's Forgotten Fame*"

JACK RUSSELL'S ARTIFACTS — RE-ESTABLISHING TIES

After having attended the naval centennial celebrations with his family, Jack Russell decided to donate some items from his war service to the Oakville Museum. Among the items given was the lighter he received as a Christmas gift from the town of Oakville. One cannot help but acknowledge the completeness of having donated such an item back to the town whose inhabitants had originally given it: after 60 years one of those lighters have found their way back home to Oakville. In an odd turn of events, a sailor, who had received gifts from the town whose people so warmly supported him, in turn, gave a gift of his own back.

I asked Jack during an interview about some of the items he donated from his time aboard HMCS *Oakville*. My specific interest was with the connection he and his shipmates felt with their namesake town. It is clear that the town of Oakville certainly felt a strong connection to their ship, but I wanted to hear from Jack what he felt and thought about the town's support.

I start by asking about a pennant that was given to the museum along with his uniform, lighter, and picture of himself at the tender age of 18. It's the pennant that puzzles me. It's small — the typical size of a yacht club pennant one would see adorning shrouds and lines of sailboats occupying slips at any waterfront town. A naval pennant would, naturally, be much larger. In addition, the picture, font, and image represented on the pennant are odd, as they do not conform to any naval pattern I could find. It is in remarkably good shape, which had me doubting if the item was something that Jack came by after his time at sea, rather than an actual artifact from the ship. To answer my question, Jack explains *Oakville*'s canteen system.

"We had a good canteen on the *Oakville*," Jack begins. He tells me that it was run by one of the NCOs and, astonishingly, he even describes its exact location aboard the ship: "it was located, after the fo'c'sle extension, just outside the galley where the cook kept himself, roughly amidships on the port side."

I find it amazing, after nearly 60 years, the clarity with he recalls the ship; then again, it was his home for several years, and unlike many other sailors in the fleet, he was not moved from ship to ship during his service. The canteen usually sold toiletries, such as soap, toothpaste, and deodorant, and, of course, cigarettes, which was the biggest seller for the canteen manager. David Francis Stewart recalls the canteen aboard his ship: "the canteen was a little hole in the wall and guys lived out

The ship's pennant obtained through redeeming a voucher at the ship's canteen. It is in remarkable condition and looks as new as the day it was made. (*Courtesy Carolyn Cross.*)

of it on chocolate, gum and pops." The canteen manager was an enterprising sort and "would cut your hair for 25 cents — worst haircut you'd ever get." There were also special snacks that the canteen would sell, which were acquired from local ports (such as New York). On special occasions, when the canteen accumulated a small profit, the crew would be given a voucher in recognition of their support. The voucher could be for anything from five, to seven, to ten dollars, and could be redeemed to buy items back from the canteen. It was on one such occasion that Jack remembered being given a voucher for Christmas in 1944. He redeemed it for a small ship's pennant.

In the hoist is a light, sky-blue anchor adorned by the White Ensign that obscures part of the stock and shank. A white chain hangs from the eye and trails behind the portside profile of a small corvette. The ship fits in the space between the throat, fluke, shank, and arm of the anchor. It is white, with waves around its base and steam flowing from its stack, also shown in white. In the fly of the pennant is the ship's name: H.M.C.S. OAKVILLE. The backdrop is gold, the edges of the fly a light blue (of the same material as the name) and red, and the hoist is green. It is one-sided and clearly handcrafted — there are no means to attach it to a line (eyes or shackles), nor is the material of the kind that could suffer the weathering of the elements. It is very clearly meant as a memento, to be displayed indoors.

It is uncertain how the pennants were obtained. Jack's first instinct is to say someone in the town of Oakville made them: "Someone from the town or its navy club," he says. He believes they were sent down as a gift for the crew, to be issued through the canteen. Then again, they could have also just as easily been contracted by the canteen officer at one of their many ports of call to be sold to crewmembers, and Jack just happened to use his voucher to obtain his. Unfortunately, the answer is not known, but the item is still an interesting artifact and tangible connection between the ship and the present.

I find the explanation of the canteen interesting as it mirrors very much how canteens are run in the Sea Cadet corps today. Often they sell snacks and items (such as mugs embossed with the corps' crest), the proceeds going back into supporting corps activities and/or items for the cadets.

Jack then tells me more about the ship's connection with the town of Oakville. The people from "Oakville and Navy Club were real pals for us," he explains. The ship actually had need of a washing machine to assist the crew in cleaning their clothes. Salt from the ocean would get into the uniform and make it stiff and rough. The men wanted to keep their clothes as clean as possible, especially when the ship berthed at one of its various ports of call (as they were required to be in uniform when on leave). Somehow, this need was communicated back to the town of Oakville, who quickly arranged to purchase a washing machine for their beloved ship. While in Halifax, the washing machine arrived care of the ship's namesake town. Jack remembers where it was located aboard ship — next to the heads. It was a sturdy regular-sized washing machine for the time, and handled their needs well.

Jack Russell. (*Courtesy Jack Russell.*)

The crew thought the town of Oakville was "the real deal that they would be so generous with us because there'd be lots of ships that didn't have a town connection … not that I know of, but Oakville was always a moneyed town and was able to support."

The town was also in the habit of sending the crewmembers "care packages" with various goodies, particularly at special times of the year.

According to Ed Stewart, veterans back in the day told him that the town even helped to establish a coke machine on board the ship. One wonders if any other ship in the fleet benefited from such close ties to a populace back home.

After the festivities surrounding the christening of *Oakville*, which many of the crew noted several weeks later had left them "… still a little dizzy from the reception given them by the people of Oakville," one sailor expressed his admiration for the town and their support. Pulling at the sleeve of his woolen jumper that he, along with the whole crew, had received as gifts, he said: "Look at this sweater. They gave one to every man on the boat and there isn't anything they could have given us that would have been more useful and acceptable. Believe me, we men here will never forget what thy [sic] did for us at Oakville."[55]

And based on the comments made by Jack Russell, echoed by his shipmates in their return letters to the Oakville Navy League's invitation to the Naval Crown Inaugural Ball, it is clear that these veterans certainly never did forget the support given to them by their ship's namesake town.

LIVING SPIRIT

Does a ship have a spirit? It's something that could be easily argued. Personally, I've always believed that a ship does have a soul, though it is born from the shared experiences of the sailors who served aboard the vessel. Their hardships, victories, toils, and successes create a unique quality that can be felt when boarding a vessel, and I would think that the sailors who served aboard *Oakville* would agree.

In passing the torch, the very spirit of the ship seems to have been transferred to the Sea Cadet Corps that proudly bears her name. Over the past decade, a slew of cadets from RCSCC *Oakville* have been the recipients of some high honours. From scholarships, international exchange opportunities, and awards, the Oakville Sea Cadets have carried on a proud tradition of excellence started by its namesake ship. Its tradition of heroism is also alive and well. In 2002, Katherine Dermott was awarded the Cadet Certificate of Commendation, the second highest award in the national cadet honours program, for her quick and decisive action as a first responder to a severely injured rock climber. She had been participating in a joint abseil exercise when she saw a civilian climber collapse after a rock fell and struck him in the head. A memorandum released by the region reads:

OAKVILLE CADET CREDITED WITH HELPING TO SAVE A LIFE

CFB Borden, Ont. — Members of Royal Canadian Sea Cadet Corps (RCSCC) *OAKVILLE* were participating in a joint training weekend with 440 Royal Canadian Army Cadet Corps at Rattlesnake Point Conservation Area, west of Toronto on Sunday, September 19, 2004. During the abseil exercises, Cadet Petty Officer 2nd Class (PO2) Katherine Dermott completed her descent down the cliff wall and was standing back in a safety zone waiting for the next cadet to descend so they could walk back in pairs. While waiting at the bottom of the rock face, she saw a rock come off the cliff and strike a civilian rock climber in the head causing him to collapse. This climber had removed his helmet.

Cadet PO2 Katherine Dermott moved immediately to the injured civilian, knelt down, and quickly assessed the nature of the injury. She offered assistance, identifying herself as a first aider. Once the other civilian students and their climbing instructor realized what was happening they took over first aid. Dermott was then asked by the civilian climbing instructor to retrieve the civilian group's first aid kit from a large black backpack, open it and be available to provided additional assistance. She noticed a man trying to open the first aid kit who was having difficulty, she asked for the first aid kit opened it and passed bandages to the civilian instructor. Cadet PO2 Dermott then collected information on the injured individual i.e. his age and other perti-

nent information. She then relayed this to the Cadet officers at the top the rock face who had called 911 using their cell phone and were talking to EMS personnel.

Dermott stayed with the injured party, and then when directed, made her way approximately one hundred and fifty metres along the jagged base of the rock face [to] meet arriving paramedics and fire dept rescue personnel and direct them to the injured man. Cadet PO2 Dermott then waited for additional EMS personnel, directing them as well to the site. The Milton Fire Department then arrived, but headed in the wrong direction, away from the accident scene. Der-

Deputy Regional Cadet Officer LCol Marcel Parisien (*left*) made the presentation to Katherine Dermott. (*Courtesy Walter Dermott.*)

mott acted quickly to redirect them, and when she was ignored, forcefully interjected herself, ensuring that they headed in the right direction. This resulted in the casualty receiving quicker lifesaving treatment.

During the course of the incident Cadet PO2 Katherine Dermott was able to maintain a high level of composure and leadership, even though she witnessed a traumatic injury to another climber. She was able to perform competently with a sense of purpose, utilizing the skills taught to her through the Sea Cadet Program within the Canadian Cadet Movement.

A Cadet Certificate of Commendation will be presented to Cadet PO2 Dermott on **Wednesday evening, March 2 at 7:30 p.m.** at RCSCC *OAKVILLE*'s Headquarters.

She was not the only cadet to distinguish herself — many others assisted in the rescue process, relaying messages, transporting gear, and directing emergency personnel. Once again, when the need for decisive action arose, *Oakville*'s response was "ready, aye, ready."

In 2013 the CO of HMCS *Ontario*, a sea cadet summer training centre, asked officers in the area to nominate former sea cadets to name their service whalers after. The summer camp had recently refurbished their fleet and the idea was to name them after people in the Royal Canadian Sea Cadet program who had distinguished themselves by an act of bravery or meritorious service. In the communication, it was specified that the nominees should be people who had been awarded any national award for bravery, cadet award of bravery, Royal Canadian Human Association Medal of Bravery, Cadet Certificate of Commendation, and/or the Navy League Award of Commendation.

The "Heroes and Whalers" initiative naturally caught my attention, as Katherine met the criteria. Working with Lt(N) Bryan McIntyre CD and Lt(N) Walter Dermott (Katherine's father and a former officer with RCSCC *Oakville*), we submitted Katherine Dermott's name for consideration. On July 14, 2013, during a naming ceremony held at HMCS *Ontario*, over a dozen former and current sea cadets were honoured. As reported in the *Kingston Whig-Standard*, "On a pier overlooking Navy Bay on the grounds of the Royal Military College on Sunday morning, a fleet of 17, 27-foot vessels sailed past a group of people gathered to mark the christening of the ships, used to train cadets during a summer training program."[56] One was named "CPO2 Katherine Dermott" (CPO2 is the abbreviation for Chief Petty Officer Second Class, which was the highest rank that Katherine reached as a Sea Cadet before retiring from the system). The article also made note that "a former cadet, 23-year-old Katherine Dermott, was also honoured for providing life-saving first aid to an injured climber in February 2005. Dermott, an Ottawa resident, was also present during the ceremony."[57]

Perhaps an even greater testament to the spirit of *Oakville* is the success rate for those cadets who graduate from the corps. Some have gone into the military and the Royal Military College. Others have enrolled in various post-secondary programs in universities and colleges across the nation. Former Cadet Chief Petty Officer First Class Zachary Reed is currently a lieutenant in the RCN and served aboard HMCS *Charlottetown* when it assisted in the NATO's Operation Unified Protector during the 2011 Libyan civil war. He makes a point to visit RCSCC *Oakville* and speak to the cadets about his experiences, motivate them to obtain their future goals, and to impress upon them the importance of the name *Oakville*, a legacy they will each carry on into the future.

They all share something in common — a spirit to achieve success and strive for their dreams. As instructors, it is the most rewarding aspect of our vocation. The officers of the corps are also due some recognition, for it is through their selfless devotion that the corps has endured the spirit of excellence that has benefited so many youth throughout the years. They volunteer countless hours a year, on top of their primary employment and family responsibilities, spending time training and working with cadets.

Though the remains of the actual ship are lost, in some way it doesn't matter. The soul of *Oakville* — the lifeblood that was the character and essence of that ship — still remains in the community from which its journey began. The truth is that *Oakville* is alive and well, continuing to faithfully serve the country and community she so valiantly fought for.

Lt(N) Zachary Reed (*right*) beside Sean Livingston. (*Courtesy Sean E. Livingston.*)

APPENDIX A
HMCS/RCSCC *Oakville* Commanding Officers

COMMANDING OFFICERS OF HMCS *OAKVILLE*

Lieutenant A.C. Jones RCNR: November 18, 1941 —
May 11, 1942

Lieutenant-Commander C.A. King DSC, RCNR:
May 12, 1942 — April 21, 1943

Lieutenant H.F. Farncombe RCNVR: April 22, 1943
— October 22, 1944

Lieutenant M.A. Griffiths RCNVR: October 23, 1944
— July 16, 1945

COMMANDING OFFICERS OF RCSCC *OAKVILLE*

Lieutenant (Navy) Rachel Capp: November 1999 —
May 2002

Lieutenant (Navy) Hank Roossien CD: May 2002 —
December 2003

Lieutenant (Navy) Bryan McIntyre: December 2003
— May 2007

Lieutenant (Navy) Lou Taddeo CD: May 2007 —
September 2009

Lieutenant (Navy) Star Edwards: September 2009 —
March 2011

Lieutenant (Navy) Bryan McIntyre CD: March 2011
— May 2014

Lieutenant (Navy) Sean E. Livingston CD: May 2014
— Present

APPENDIX B
RCSCC *OAKVILLE* COXSWAINS

Cadet Chief Petty Officer 2nd Class Jennifer Gignac: November 1999 — May 2000

Cadet Chief Petty Officer 1st Class Kevin McIntyre: May 2000 — May 2002

Cadet Chief Petty Officer 1st Class Mark Pyza: May 2002 — May 2003

Cadet Chief Petty Officer 2nd Class Colin Hoult: May 2003 — June 2003

Cadet Chief Petty Officer 1st Class Kevin McIntyre: June 2003 — October 2003

Cadet Chief Petty Officer 1st Class Ashlea Watson: October 2003 — May 2004

Cadet Chief Petty Officer 1st Class Shane Stephenson: May 2004 — May 2005

Cadet Chief Petty Officer 1st Class Zachary Reed: May 2005 — May 2006

Cadet Chief Petty Officer 2nd Class Katherine Dermott: May 2006 — May 2007

Cadet Chief Petty Officer 1st Class Joshua Reed: May 2007 — May 2008

Cadet Chief Petty Officer 1st Class Victoria Reed: May 2008 — May 2009

Cadet Chief Petty Officer 1st Class Emily Wilson: May 2009 — February 2010

Cadet Chief Petty Officer 2nd Class Hansel Paico: March 2010 — May 2011

Cadet Chief Petty Officer 1st Class Christopher Chung: May 2011 — June 2012

Cadet Chief Petty Officer 1st Class Benjamin Marshall: June 2012 — Present

GLOSSARY
of Selected Military/Naval Terms and Abbreviations

A20	Douglas A20 Havoc Light Bomber
AB	Able Seaman
Adm	Admiral
CAF	Canadian Armed Forces
Capt	Captain (Canadian Army and Royal Canadian Air Force)
Capt(N)	Captain (Navy)
CARIBSEAFRON	Caribbean Sea Frontier
CCM	Canadian Cadet Movement
CD	Canadian Forces Decoration
Cdr	Commander
C/ERA	Chief Engine Room Artificer
C/ERA3	Chief Engine Room Artificer III
CFB	Canadian Forces Base
CIC	Cadet Instructor Cadre
CO	Commanding Officer
COATS	Cadet Organizations Administrative and Training Service
Coder or Cdr.	Ordinary Coder (in the current RCN "Cdr" refers solely to the rank of Commander)
Col	Colonel
Cook or CK(S)	Cook
CPO	Chief Petty Officer
CPO1	Chief Petty Officer 1st Class
CPO2	Chief Petty Officer 2nd Class
CNS	Chief of Naval Staff
DND	Department of National Defence
DSC	Distinguished Service Cross
DSM	Distinguished Service Medal
DSO	Distinguished Service Order
ERA	Engine Room Artificer
ERA3	Engine Room Artificer III
ERA4	Engine Room Artificer IV
HMCS	His/Her Majesty's Canadian Ship
HMS	His/Her Majesty's Ship
HA	Halifax to Aruba
HX	Halifax to United Kingdom
KN	Key West to New York
Ldg/Ck.	Leading Cook
LCdr	Lieutenant-Commander

LCol	Lieutenant-Colonel		RAdm	Rear-Admiral
Ldg. Sea. or Ldg/Sea.	Leading Seaman		RCAC	Royal Canadian Air Cadets
Ldg. Sig. or Ldg/Sig.	Leading Signalman		RCN	Royal Canadian Navy
Ldg. Sto. or Ldg/Sto.	Leading Stoker		RCNR	Royal Canadian Naval Reserve
Ldg. Tel.	Leading Telegraphist		RCNVR	Royal Canadian Naval Volunteer Reserve
LSA	Leading Supply Assistant		RCSCC	Royal Canadian Sea Cadet Corps
LSBA	Leading Sick Bert Attendant		RN	Royal Navy
Lt. or Lieu	Lieutenant		RNR	Royal Naval Reserves
Lieut. Comdr.	old abbreviation of "Lieutenant-Commander"		SA	Supply Assistant
Lt-Gov.	Lieutenant Governor		SBA	Sick Berth Attendant
Lt(N)	Lieutenant (Navy)		SBStJ	The Most Venerable Order of the Hospital of St. John of Jerusalem (Serving Brother grade)
Maj	Major			
MC	Military Cross		Sig.	Signalman
MMM	Member of the Order of Military Merit		SLt, S/Lt, or Sub. Lieut	Sub-Lieutenant
NEF	Newfoundland Escort Force		SPO	Stoker Petty Officer
NO	Navigation Officer		Sto	Stoker
NOAC	Naval Officers Association of Canada		Sto. I	Stoker I
OBE	Order of the British Empire		Sto. II	Stoker II
Old Man	Naval Slang for the Captain of a ship		Stwd.	Steward
ONS	Liverpool to Halifax, Slow		TAG	Trinidad, Aruba, Guantanamo
OOW	Officer of the Watch		TAW	Trinidad, Aruba, Key West
OD or Ord. Sea.	Ordinary Seaman (the "Ord. Sea." abbreviation may have been written this way to avoid confusion with the abbreviation "OS")		Tel.	Telegraphist
			USN	United States Navy
			VAdm	Vice-Admiral
OS	Officer Steward (in the current RCN "OS" refers to Ordinary Seaman)		WLEF	Western Local Escort Force
			WRNS	Women's Royal Naval Service
O/Sig.	Ordinary Signalman		XO	Executive Officer
PBY	Patrol Bomber Consolidated Aircraft			
PC	Patrol Costal Ship			
PCS	Patrol Craft, Submarine			
PO	Petty Officer			
PO1	Petty Officer 1st Class			
PO2	Petty Officer 2nd Class			

ENDNOTES

PREFACE: DISCOVERING "*OAKVILLE*"

1. Papers focused heavily on the historic importance of this day, as did the programme published for the christening ceremony. Mayor Deans was quoted in the *Telegram*: "Christen Corvette 'Oakville' As Entire Town Watches," *Toronto Evening Telegram*, November 6, 1941: 4.

CHAPTER 1: CHEAP AND NASTY

1. The Diaries of William Lyon Mackenzie King, Thursday, May 27, 1937: 2.
2. Department of National Defence: Canadian Forces Navy Seamanship Handbook, 1977 (1–11, CFP 152).
3. Correlli Barnett, *Engage the Enemy More Closely: The Royal Navy in the Second World War* (New York: W.W. Norton & Co Inc., 1991), 460. Comments made by Britain's First Sea Lord on March 5, 1942, indicating that if the U-boat offensive succeeded, soldiers and supplies would not be able to be ferried across to Britain to prepare for an invasion of Western Europe.
4. John Terraine, *Business in Great Waters: The U-Boat Wars, 1916–1945* (London: Leo Cooper, 1989), 467.

Order was given by Adolf Hitler on January 3, 1942.
5. Taken from a letter sent by the UK Secretary of State for Foreign Affairs, Samuel Hoare, to the German Ambassador in London, June 18, 1935, section 2, sub-section F.
6. Michael L. Hadley, *U-Boats Against Canada: German Submarines in Canadian Waters* (Kingston: McGill-Queen's University Press, 1985), 11.
7. William Arthur Bishop, *True Canadian Heroes at Sea* (Toronto: Prospero Publishing, 2006), 28. The First Sea Lord in this case was Winston Churchill.
8. Winston S. Churchill, *Their Finest Hour* (Boston: Houghton Mifflin Company, 1949), 529.
9. Tony German, *The Sea Is at Our Gates: The History of the Canadian Navy* (Toronto: McClelland & Stewart, 1990), 71.
10. Marc Milner, *North Atlantic Run: The Royal Canadian Navy and the Battle for the Convoys* (Toronto: University of Toronto Press, 1985), 22.
11. *Ibid.*, 15.
12. J.L. Granatstein, *Canada's War: The Politics of the Mackenzie King Government, 1939–1945* (Toronto: Oxford University Press, 1975), 19.
13. Milner, *North Atlantic Run*, 79.
14. Bishop, *True Canadian Heroes at Sea*, 28.
15. Marc Milner, "The Humble Corvette: Part 27," *Legion Magazine*, June 5, 2008, *http://legionmagazine.com/en/2008/06/the-humble-corvette-navy-part-27/*. Accessed December 8, 2013. Milner explains why Churchill chose an unthreatening name and designation for these

vessels, indicating that he "… wanted to give the little ships names rather than numbers, and thought it would be good public relations to report that one of Hitler's sea wolves (U-boats) had been destroyed by a vessel named for a flower, like His Majesty's Ship Buttercup. So the Royal Navy dubbed the new ships 'Flower-class corvettes' and gave them all names like Hibiscus and Poppy."

16. *Ibid.*
17. R. Douglas Francis, Richard Jones, and Donald B. Smith, *Destinies: Canadian History Since Confederation* (Scarborough: Nelson Thomson Learning, 2000), 318.
18. David Francis Stewart, Interview by Sean E. Livingston (Verbal), Grimsby, Ontario, November 24, 2013. David lied about his age when he joined the navy. He was 16, but said he was 18, and since he was a Sea Cadet (as were his two eldest brothers), the recruiter jumped at the chance to enroll them: "When you said you were a sea cadet 'they grabbed you' because of their training." In fact, the Cadets actually trained RCNVR sailors on the use of the field cannon at HMCS *Star*.
19. *Ibid.*
20. Mac Johnston, *Corvettes Canada: Convoy Veterans of WWII Tell Their True Stories* (Toronto: McGraw-Hill Ryerson, 1994), 127.
21. Jack Russell, Interview by Sean E. Livingston (Telephone), Burlington-Sarnia, Ontario, November 9, 2013.
22. *Ibid.*
23. *Ibid.*
24. *Ibid.*
25. David Francis Stewart.
26. *Ibid.*
27. *Ibid.*
28. *Ibid.* When David was sent off to Quebec to do his communications course, it was the longest course in the RCN. As he said during our interview, "… gunner six weeks, radar six weeks as well, but the communications was 18 weeks long and all heavy studying." He remembered thinking to himself, "Hell, I quit high school because I didn't like studying!" When he went to the recruiting office in Hamilton, the recruitment officer had asked, "What do you want to be?" David had wanted to be a gunner like his older brother, but the recruiter replied, "We have enough gunners. Drafting for signalmen." David thought of it and mentioned that his other brother, Bill, was a signalman. That was it — the recruiter said "you're a signalman then." David still regrets having said that: "It was the worst choice of trade to be in the navy!"
29. Jack Russell. Roughly 15 years ago Jack took a cruise. Decades after his service in the RCNVR, he wanted to re-experience what it was like on a ship, and, as he admitted, to see if he'd be seasick again. Although he was happy to see that he still had his sea legs and was able to enjoy the vacation, the experience was altogether different from sailing in a corvette. Aboard the colossal cruise ship, "you could hardly feel a ripple," he explained.
30. Tina Depko-Denver, "Veteran Recounts Life Aboard HMCS Galt," *Burlington Post*, November 8, 2013: 8.
31. David Francis Stewart. HMCS *Stellarton* was a modified Flower-class corvette with an extended fo'c'sle.
32. Jack Russell.
33. David Francis Stewart.
34. Jack Russell.
35. David Francis Stewart.
36. Jack Russell.
37. Tina Depko-Denver, "Veteran Recounts Life Aboard HMCS Galt," 8.
38. Jack Russell.
39. Alex Bramson, Interview by Sean E. Livingston (Verbal), Burlington, Ontario, October 12, 2010.
40. David Francis Stewart.
41. *Ibid.*
42. *Ibid.*
43. *Ibid.*
44. Alex Bramson. Jack Russell recalls that Ben Carson was a "big fella and over six foot-tall, slim and could put me under his arm — I only weighed about 118 pounds — and carry me around the mess deck." Jack laughed at the memory during our interview, adding: "He was the guy, if any trouble happened, who would go to bat for ya."
45. Jack Russell.
46. Milner, "The Humble Corvette: Part 27."
47. Milner, *North Atlantic Run*, 40.
48. Marc Milner, *Canada's Navy: The First Century* (Toronto: University of Toronto Press, 1999), 97.
49. *Ibid.*, 138.
50. *Ibid.*
51. Bishop, *True Canadian Heroes at Sea*, 27; Milner, *Canada's Navy*, 157.
52. Marine Museum of the Great Lakes at Kingston, "Port Arthur Shipbuilding Finds Records Group 5," *www.marmuseum.ca/finding_aids/Port_Arthur_Shipbuilding_Finding_Aid[1].pdf*. Accessed December 8, 2013.
53. Portions referenced from Helgason, Gudmundur, "Flower Class Corvettes," *www.uboat.net/allies/warships/class.html?ID=42*, last modified December 5, 2013. Accessed December 8, 2013. *Uboat.net* is an excellent example of a well-referenced online resource for Second World War nautical information.
54. Oakville Historical Society (OHS) document

supplied by Lt. Cdr Kenneth B. Culley RCNVR, XO of HMCS *Oakville*.

55. Johnston, *Corvettes Canada*, 214.
56. Milner, *Canada's Navy*, 91.
57. OHS information sheet supplied by Lt. Cdr Kenneth B. Culley.
58. OHS information sheet as well as picture of Ordinary Seaman Douglas Maclean. Lawrence and Gaylord's works (cited below) on the U94 encounter also make mention of this.
59. Johnston, *Corvettes Canada*, 232
60. Milner, in his article "The Humble Corvette: Part 27," explains that British Corvettes had the galley positioned aft of the engine room, which meant that crewmen had to walk on the open deck, food in hand, to reach their respective messes towards the bow of the ship.
61. Letter from Kenneth Culley to Elaine Nielsen, September 10, 1999.

CHAPTER 2: A GLIMMER OF HOPE

1. "Oakville Plans Great Ceremony for Christening," the *Hamilton Spectator*, October 25, 1941.
2. The article notes that the date for the ceremony had been shifted to Wednesday — the original date for the ceremony is not mentioned.
3. Omitted from the article is Jack (Jock) Gairdner, from Appleby College, who must have been added later. He does appear in the ceremony programme (name spelled "Jock"), as well as in press coverage of the day.
4. Article mistakenly refers to him as a lieutenant-commander.
5. "Oakville Plans Great Ceremony for Christening," October 25, 1941.
6. *Ibid.*
7. "Oakville Agog As Day Nears for Ceremony," *Toronto Evening Telegram*, November 4, 1941: 6.
8. *Ibid.*
9. *Ibid.*
10. *Ibid.* Lakeside Park is at the southernmost end of Navy Street in Oakville. The agenda for the ceremony was listed in full in the paper, even the banquet and toasts.
11. *Ibid.*
12. Although they are not mentioned, it stands to reason that all youth organizations that were present at the ceremony would have attended as well (e.g. Boy Scouts, Girl Guides, Cubs, and school children.)
13. John Blatherwick, "Awards to the Royal Canadian Navy," *www.rcnvr.com/N-RCN-WW2.php*, last

modified July 20, 2001. Accessed December 8, 2013. This is a wonderful site created by retired Commander Francis John Blatherwick, CM, CStJ, OBC, CD, MD, author, and notably the longest serving medical officer in the CAF (upon his retirement in 2000). The site is well researched and provides detailed documentation/service records for many decorated RCN, RCNR, and RCNVR sailors (among others). He is presently the honourary colonel for 12 (Vancouver) Field Ambulance.

14. Juno Beach Centre, "Admiral P.W. Nelles," *www.junobeach.org/e/3/can-pep-can-nelles-e.htm*. Accessed December 8, 2013.
15. Bishop, *True Canadian Heroes at Sea*, 25.
16. Ian McKay, "Tartanism Triumphant": *Acadiensis*, XXI, No. 2 (1992): 17, *http://journals.hil.unb.ca/index.php/Acadiensis/article/view/11913/0*. Accessed December 8, 2013.
17. T. Stephen Henderson, *Angus L. Macdonald: A Provincial Liberal* (Toronto: University of Toronto Press, 2007), 17–20.
18. *Ibid.*, 54. Joseph Howe, the famous Liberal reformer, was responsible for obtaining responsible government for Nova Scotia in 1848, the first province in Canada to do so.
19. McKay, "Tartanism Triumphant," 20. McKay's article actually argues that Macdonald constructed Nova Scotia's apparent Scottish lineage and states that the province never actually had strong Scottish roots.
20. Henderson, *Angus L. Macdonald*, 85
21. Geoffrey Stevens, *Stanfield* (Toronto: McClelland & Stewart, 1973), 45–46.
22. McKay, "Tartanism Triumphant," 19.
23. *Ibid.*, 18, sourcing *Mail-Star* (Halifax), April 13, 1954.
24. *Ibid.*, 17–18.
25. One other event drew large crowds as well. Sub-Lieutenant Harold Lawrence and Stoker Petty Officer Arthur Powell were paraded as heroes in the town after *Oakville* had sunk U94.
26. Mr. Shaw's hardcopy account is located in the OHS Archives. His letter appeared in the local newspaper, the *Oakville Beaver*, in November 1981. This is the only account that mentions that the organizations present at the reception actually marched to the ceremony before performing a March Past for Macdonald. Thus, some of the pictures presented in this book may be of the first march to Lakeside Park, and not of the actual March Past (with the obvious exception of those images that show the platform in front of the old post office.)
27. "Thousands Pack Shoreline for Oakville's Christening," *Toronto Daily Star*, November 6, 1941: 8.
28. "Christening and Reception HMCS Oakville," referenced from an original copy of the Ceremony Programme, November 5, 1941.

29. The *Globe and Mail* also included an image of Nelles and Macdonald inspecting members of the Toronto and Hamilton RCNVR, and surprisingly refers to it as the guard of honour. This is probably because the uniforms worn by Sea Cadets were identical to the non-commissioned naval personnel. In fact, the only way of distinguishing reservist from cadet in the pictures is to note whether the group is wearing ceremonial belts, leggings, and bearing arms fixed with bayonets. This manner of dress is specific to honour guards. Thus, it can be concluded that since the RCNVR detachments are dressed in honorary attire that the guard of honour was in fact made up of the reservists from Toronto and Hamilton, and not the Sea Cadets. It also appears that the Australians played a similar role.

30. "Thousands Pack Shoreline for Oakville's Christening," 8.

31. Ceremony Programme, 6.

32. "Admiral Nelles Warns of Subs Off N. Scotia," the *Evening Citizen*, November 6, 1941: 2.

33. *Ibid.*

34. "Thousands Pack Shoreline for Oakville's Christening," 8; Songs sung are listed in the Ceremony Programme, 4.

35. *Ibid.*

36. "Thousands Pack Shoreline for Oakville's Christening," 8.

37. Oddly, only the *Star* makes note of the plane salute. This would have been significant — since the vast majority of ships produced in Canada for the war were corvettes, it is obvious that not all could receive such an honour (not to mention having both Nelles and Macdonald present at the christening.)

38. "Oakville Agog As Day Nears for Ceremony," 6.

39. "HMCS Oakville Ready as Nazi Submarines Lurk Near," *Globe and Mail*, November 6, 1941: 8.

40. P.J. Philip, "U-Boats Roaming Labrador Coast," *New York Times*, November 6, 1941: 1; Reuters, "U-Boats attacked off Newfoundland," *London Times*, November 6, 1941, 6. Both sources have coverage, although the *New York Times* is more extensive.

41. "U-Boats Roaming Labrador Coast," 1.

42. *Ibid.*

43. "Oakville Agog As Day Nears for Ceremony," 4.

44. Staff, "Attacked Wherever They Come," *Globe and Mail*, November 6, 1941, 4.

45. "Thousands Pack Shoreline for Oakville's Christening," 8.

46. The only notable comparison, ironically, is the parade held in honour of HMCS *Oakville*'s heroes in 1942.

47. *Hamilton Spectator*, November 6, 1941, 1.

48. "Oakville Agog As Day Nears for Ceremony," 4.

49. *Hamilton Spectator*, November 6, 1941, 1.

50. "Thousands Pack Shoreline for Oakville's Christening," 8.

51. Letter, Kenneth Culley to Linda Gignac, President of Oakville Navy League, September 11, 2000.

52. "War Hero in Legendary Battle with German Sub," *National Post*, May 16, 2002. In fact, HMCS *Oakville* had wooden gun placements, which mimicked the actual guns she would receive on the coast.

53. Johnston, *Corvettes Canada*, 68.

54. *Ibid.*

CHAPTER 3: DOGS AND WOLVES

1. Johnston, *Corvettes Canada*, 98.

2. *Ibid.*, 150.

3. *Ibid.*

4. Name also appears as "Kuppisch."

5. "Herbert Kuppisch," *uboat.net*.

6. "Otto Ites," *uboat.net*.

7. "Newbury," *uboat.net*.

8. "San Florentino," *uboat.net*.

9. Gaylord T.M. Kelshall, *The U-Boat War in the Caribbean* (Annapolis, MD: Naval Institute Press, 1994), 155.

10. *Ibid.*, 156.

11. *Ibid.*

12. "Amakura," *uboat.net*.

13. Kelshall, *The U-Boat War in the Caribbean*, 156.

14. Ibid., 156.

15. Earnest J. King, "First Report to the Secretary of the Navy: Covering Our Peacetime Navy and Our Wartime Navy and Including Combat Operations up to 1 March 1944," April 1944: 75–88. Admiral Ernest J. King was the Commander in Chief, United States Fleet, and Chief of Naval Operations.

16. Some sources state that Oakville was stationed at the Port Quarter while other sources indicate it was stationed at the Port Beam.

17. Letter from Don Mann, a.k.a. Donald N. Mackirdy, to Linda Gignac, January 8, 2000.

18. Hal Lawrence, *Tales of the North Atlantic* (Toronto: McClelland & Stewart, 1985), 152.

19. Johnston, *Corvettes Canada*, 270.

20. Canadian Naval Forces Interview with Culley, 2.

21. Lawrence, *Tales of the North Atlantic*, 153.

22. Johnston, *Corvettes Canada*, 152.

23. *Ibid.*

24. Lawrence, *Tales of the North Atlantic*, 153.

25. Both Adams and MacLean displayed incredible marksmanship. Unlike a sniper on firm ground, these men pulled off expert shots on a moving vessel, rocking in force 4 waters.

26. Gordon Sinclair, *Toronto Daily Star*, November 10, 1942: 10.
27. Hal Lawrence, *A Bloody War* (Toronto: McClelland & Stewart, 1979), 87.
28. In his interview, Powell mentions little of this incident — only that he was there and suffered a shattered eardrum. Other parts of his statement seem disjointed — he seems to believe that he and Lawrence correctly guessed the side of the ship the U-boat would emerge and explains that the other members were not present because they had mustered on the opposite side of the ship. He oddly notes that both he and Lawrence stripped off their clothing, as they expected to swim to the U-boat.
29. It was a serious threat, one taken to heart by the RCN. David F. Stewart remembers that signal books aboard ship had thick lead covers (he feels it could have been half-inch thick!) They had canvas bags so that, in the event of their vessel being captured by the enemy, they could put their signal books into the bags and toss them over the side, thus ensuring that the signals remained secret and out of the hands of the enemy.
30. Lawrence, *Tales of the North Atlantic*, 157.
31. *Ibid.*
32. Lawrence, *A Bloody War*, 88.
33. *Ibid.*
34. Kelshall, *The U-Boat War in the Caribbean*, 161.
35. Lawrence referred to it as "Death Spasms."
36. Kelshall, *The U-Boat War in the Caribbean*, 158.
37. Adam Mayers, "WWII's Unsung Heroes," *Toronto Star*, August 3, 2006: R2.
38. Not surprising that *Oakville* requested that *Lea* assist the boarding party, as the corvette was busy tending to its own wounds, which, undoubtedly, would have made any strenuous maneuvers difficult. Its boats were in the water though, on way to assist the boarding party and would rescue some of the German crew.
39. Lawrence, *Tales of the North Atlantic*, 159.
40. Sinclair, *Toronto Daily Star*, 10.
41. Kelshall, *The U-Boat War in the Caribbean*, 160; "San Fabian," *uboat.net*.
42. "Esso Aruba," *uboat.net*.
43. Written as Lea to JVB. Error in transcript.
44. Kelshall, *The U-Boat War in the Caribbean*, 161.
45. Aside from those noted in the text or endnotes, the following were also drawn upon to help me paint the picture of the TAW-15 battle:

- Canadian Naval Forces Memorandum to the Naval Broadcasting officer, "Re: Recent action of H.M.C.S. "Oakville" Interview with Lieut. Cully," August 28, 1942, 1–4.

- Canadian Naval Forces Memorandum to the Naval Broadcasting Officer, "Re: Recent Action of H.M.C.S. "Oakville" Interview with Lieut. Lawrence and Stoker Petty Officer Powell," August 28, 1942: 1–7.
- Information Bulletin from the United States Fleet, "Oakville Sinks Sub," August 28, 1942.
- Royal Canadian Navy Monthly Review, 1000-5 No. 10, October 1942.
- M.J. Ryan, "Leap Aboard Sinking Sub Pair Kill Two Nazi Seaman and Subdue Rest of Crew," *Toronto Evening Telegram*, November 10, 1942.
- Mike Ryan's "Oakville's Story": original transcript of the above, written in Halifax but not dated. It appears to be based on the eyewitness account of Lawrence, Powell, and Culley of the battle (although King is mentioned, the fact that the author omits details — example, how he moves in his seat — indicates that *Oakville*'s CO was not present).
- Royal Canadian Navy Press Release.

CHAPTER 4: FADED LEGEND

1. Gordon Sinclair was a famous Canadian journalist and reporter. During the Second World War he was noted for covering the Dieppe Raid (writing and broadcasting the story for Toronto). Sinclair was recognized for his contributions to Canada in 1979 when he was inducted as an Officer in the Order of Canada. He died in 1984.
2. Royal Canadian Navy Press Release, Naval Headquarters (Information Section), November 10, 1942: 1.
3. *Ibid.*
4. *Ibid.*, 3.
5. *The Toronto Daily Star*, December 18, 1942: 8.
6. Johnston, *Corvettes Canada*, 151.
7. *Ibid.*, 152. Charles Gowdyk's name is spelled as "Gowdyck" in this quote, but according to all other sources it appears the correct spelling was "Gowdyk."
8. Mayers, "WWII's Unsung Heroes," R2.
9. Johnston, *Corvettes Canada*, 28.
10. *Ibid.*
11. The names and titles from both the 1942 and 1943 crew pictures are presented as they appear underneath each respective photo. There likely are

some errors — in the '42 picture the abbreviation "E.R." is used but was likely meant to be "E.R.A.," while in the '43 picture Lawrence is referred to as the "X.D." rather than the "X.O.," which I believe was likely what was intended. Also, the abbreviations for military titles and terms can be found in the glossary but will appear without periods, as that is the standard form for writing them.

12. The phrase relates to sandbars that form at the mouth of many rivers and bays. Crossing the sand "bar" meant to journey off into the unknown, leaving the familiarity and relative safety of the harbour. It is also the title of a famous 1889 poem by Lord Alfred Tennyson (1809–1892).

13. Since 1968 it has been known as Canadian Forces Base (CFB) Halifax, the current home of the Atlantic Fleet. Prior to the Second World War it was under the army's control, being originally built as a British Army barracks.

14. Known as "Canada's Victorian Oil Town."

15. There was a poster on the quarterdeck indicating the codes and depths: A, for 50 feet; B, for 100 feet; C, for 125 feet, etc. David F. Stewart's first post was at the rear depth-charge racks — his specific post was to man the phone at the quarterdeck, where he would have to transmit orders from the bridge to the deck officer. "I wasn't told anything though," David recounts. "The depth charges were rolling off the stern rails while the phone rang." Feeling awkward, he picked up, saying "Hello?" A voice ordered: "Set the pattern B for baker." David was only 16 years old (he had lied about his age), and felt out of sorts shouting an order to an officer even though he was about 10 feet away and the depth charges were exploding. So he gently transmitted the order: "Set pattern B for baker." Naturally, the officer didn't hear him. When the officer finally noticed that David was trying to tell him something, he had no patience: "For Christ sakes yell it out man!" And so David did consistently after that.

16. Most U-boats were not destroyed by a direct, well-placed hit with a depth charge but rather a series of strikes that shook, and ultimately, damaged the U-boat. Many were actually able to survive hours of being bombarded by depth charges. In 1945, U427 purportedly managed to survive 678 depth charges.

17. Attempts are being made to draw more specific detail and information about this event.

18. The image omitted the description of the bottom portion of the poster.

19. "Otto Ites," *uboat.net*.

20. Johnston, *Corvettes Canada*, 274.

CHAPTER 5: THE LONG REVIVAL

1. Letter from Acting Director Norman Hillmer, Directorate of History, to Colonel Gilberto Estrella, August 26, 1981.

2. Letter from Mayor of Oakville Harry Barrett to His Excellency Victor Delascio, Ambassador for Canada from Venezuela, March 2, 1983.

3. *Ibid.*

4. *Ibid.*

5. Letter from Mayor of Oakville Harry Barrett to Mr. Jose T. Colmenares A. Col. (VAF) Venezuelan Air and Naval Attache, March 21, 1984.

6. Letter from K. R. Macpherson, Archives of Ontario, Ministry of Citizenship and Culture, to Harry Barrett, August 17, 1984.

7. *Ibid.*

8. All letters are part of Edward Stewart's collection. I am grateful for his generosity in allowing me to utilize them for this section of the book.

9. Letter from R.C. Charlton to Editor of *The Star Shell*, February 26, 1989.

10. Article by Lilian Dirisio, presented in the *Oakville Beaver*, 1989 (photocopy from Edward Stewart's collection, which omits the date).

11. Well known as "WRENS."

12. He was an honourary colonel.

13. As listed in the ceremony programme.

CHAPTER 6: PASSING THE TORCH

1. Howard Mozel, "Mystery Deepens As Sea Cadet Organizers Delve Into Past of HMCS Oakville," *Oakville Beaver*, August 4, 1999.

2. Howard Mozel, "The Exciting Effort Now Underway to Establish the Royal Canadian Sea Cadet Corps Oakville Will Pay Homage to Local History As Well As to the Future," *Oakville Beaver*, July 11, 1999.

3. *Ibid.*

4. *Ibid.*

5. *Oakville Beaver*, September 19, 1999.

6. "Gun Shields of Adopted Ship To Bear Oakville Town Crest," *Toronto Daily Star*, March 31, 1943.

7. *Ibid.*

8. *Ibid.*

9. *Ibid.*

10. Darryl Litchfield, Oakville Images: Oakville Memories New & Old, "H.M.C.S. Oakville Crest (1940s)." Accessed December 9, 2013. There is no evidence that a crest was ever installed on HMCS

Oakville. In fact, most sailors indicated they believed it never had one.

11. *Ibid.*
12. *Ibid.*
13. *Ibid.*
14. Letter to Linda Gignac from Major P.E. Lansey, September 9, 1999.
15. *Ibid.*
16. *Ibid.*
17. *Ibid.*
18. *Ibid.*
19. Guide to Naval Heraldry for Royal Canadian Sea Cadet Corps and Navy League of Canada Cadet Corps, revised January 5, 1999.
20. *Ibid.*
21. *Ibid.*
22. *Ibid.*
23. All rope borders are gold. The maple leaves at the bottom of the frame must be red for RCSCC/Navy League Cadet Corps, while they remain gold for all HMCS ships.
24. Letter from Inspector of Badges, W.A. West, to Sue Fellows, Secretary Oakville Navy League, August 31, 1999.
25. *Ibid.*
26. Amber Clarke, *Oakville Beaver*, November 10, 1999.
27. Letter from Kenneth Culley to Linda Gignac, September 11, 2000.
28. Mary Collett, "Navy Vet Shares Experiences on HMCS Oakville," *Oakville Beaver*, February 2, 2000.
29. *Ibid.*
30. *Ibid.*
31. The Oakville Navy League actually had another grand scheme: they wished to build a building in the shape of a ship along the town's lakefront near Erchless Estates, one that would be utilized by Oakville cadets of all three elements. High costs and the inevitable failure of the naval ball fundraising initiative made its construction impossible.
32. Letter from Douglas MacLean to Linda Gignac, n.d.
33. Literally means to have lived in the forecastle (fo'c'sle), rather than the quarter deck, and is a naval term to refer to seamen rather than officers. To have served before the mast is to indicate that an officer was once a junior rating before taking a commission.
34. Also known as either CERAs (if a chief) or ERAs, the Chief Engine Room Artificer was the senior

person in charge of the ship's engine and was the person who took orders from the ship's telegraph and manually adjusted the throttle of the ship.

35. Letter from Allan Mole to Linda Gignac, September 30, 2000.
36. *Ibid.*
37. Letter from Kenneth Culley to Linda Gignac, March 8, 2001.
38. *Ibid.*
39. *Ibid.*
40. Letter from Alma Lawrence to Linda Gignac, May 10, 2000.
41. *Ibid.*
42. *Ibid.*
43. According to Ed Stewart, news of the event's cancelation did not reach some of the veterans who still came down to Oakville and ended up at the Oakville Museum.
44. "War Hero in Legendary Battle with German Sub," *National Post*, May 16, 2002.
45. *Ibid.*
46. "Bell on Cairn Won't Ring Till War Ends or Ship Sunk," *Toronto Daily Star*, November 27, 1941.
47. *Ibid.*
48. There are many shipwrecks in Buzzards Bay, with a surprising amount recorded during the war era. It also was not uncommon for the wrecks to be salvaged and sold. The 76-foot tug *Neponset*, which sunk after being rammed at night by the steamer *Robert E. Lee* on December 12, 1927 (and lost two hands) was salvaged in 1928 by the Merritt-Chapman & Scott Corporation and sold at a public auction.
49. *Toronto Daily Star*, November 27, 1941.
50. *Ibid.*
51. *Ibid.*
52. *Ibid.*
53. *Ibid.*
54. Carolyn Cross email to the Author.
55. This is from a newspaper clipping collected by Ed Stewart, but unfortunately the name of the newspaper and date are not visible. From the image and age, it is clearly from the 1940s and likely from the 1941 christening.
56. Danielle VandenBrink, "Cadets Honoured for Heroics," *Kingston Whig-Standard*, July 14, 2013.
57. *Ibid.*

BIBLIOGRAPHY

Barnett, Correlli. *Engage the Enemy More Closely: The Royal Navy in the Second World War*. New York: W.W. Norton & Co Inc., 1991.

Bishop, William Arthur. *True Canadian Heroes at Sea*. Toronto: Prospero Publishing, 2006.

Churchill, Winston S. *Their Finest Hour*. Boston: Houghton Mifflin Company, 1949.

Francis, R. Douglas, Richard Jones, and Donald B. Smith. *Destinies: Canadian History Since Confederation*. Scarborough: Nelson Thomson Learning, 2000.

German, Tony. *The Sea Is at Our Gates: The History of the Canadian Navy*. Toronto: McClelland & Stewart, 1990.

Granatstein, J. L. *Canada's War: The Politics of the Mackenzie King Government, 1939–1945*. Toronto: Oxford University Press, 1975.

Hadley, Michael L. *U-Boats Against Canada: German Submarines in Canadian Waters*. Kingston: McGill-Queen's University Press, 1985.

Henderson, T. Stephen. *Angus L. Macdonald: A Provincial Liberal*. Toronto: University of Toronto Press, 2007.

Johnston, Mac. *Corvettes Canada: Convoy Veterans of WWII Tell Their True Stories*. Toronto: McGraw-Hill Ryerson, 1994.

Kelshall, Gaylord T.M. *The U-Boat War in the Caribbean*. Annapolis, MD: Naval Institute Press, 1994.

King, Earnest J. "First Report to the Secretary of the Navy: Covering our Peacetime Navy and our Wartime Navy and including combat operations up to 1 March 1944." April 1944.

Lawrence, Hal. *A Bloody War*. Toronto: McClelland & Stewart Inc., 1979.

———. *Tales of the North Atlantic*. Toronto: McClelland & Stewart, 1985.

Lynch, Thomas G. *Canada's Flowers: History of the Corvettes of Canada 1939–1945*. Halifax: Nimbus Publishing Limited, 1983.

McKay, Ian. "Tartanism Triumphant": *Acadiensis*. No. 2 (1992): 17. *http://journals.hil.unb.ca/index.php/Acadiensis/article/view/11913/0* (accessed December 8, 2013).

Milner, Marc. *Canada's Navy: The First Century*. Toronto: University of Toronto Press, 1999.

———. *North Atlantic Run: The Royal Canadian Navy and the Battle for the Convoys*. Toronto: University of Toronto Press, 1985.

———. "The Humble Corvette: Part 27." *Legion Magazine*, June 5, 2008.

Stevens, Geoffrey. *Stanfield*. Toronto: McClelland & Stewart, 1973.

Terraine, John. *Business in Great Waters: The U-Boat Wars, 1916–1945*. London: Leo Cooper, 1989.

Interviews

Bramson, Alex. Interview by Sean E. Livingston (Verbal), Burlington, Ontario, October 12, 2010.

Russell, Jack. Interview by Sean E. Livingston (Telephone), Burlington-Sarnia, Ontario, November 9, 2013.

Stewart, David Francis. Interview by Sean E. Livingston (Verbal), Grimsby, Ontario, November 24, 2013.

INDEX

ALSO FROM DUNDURN

WHITE ENSIGN FLYING

Corvette HMCS *Trentonian*
Roger Litwiller

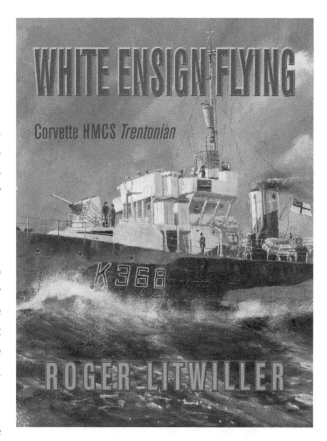

White Ensign Flying tells the story of HMCS *Trentonian*, a Canadian corvette that fought U-Boats in the Second World War. *Trentonian* escorted convoys on the North Atlantic and through the deadly waters near England and France. The ship was attacked by the Americans in a friendly-fire incident during Operation Neptune and later earned the dubious distinction of being the last corvette sunk by the enemy.

Litwiller has interviewed many of the men who served in *Trentonian* and collected their stories. Their unique personal perspectives are combined with the official record of the ship, giving an intimate insight into the life of a sailor — from the tedium of daily life in a ship at sea to the terror of fighting for your life in a sinking ship.

Over one hundred photos from the private collections of the crew and military archives bring the story of *Trentonian* to life, illustrating this testament to the ship and the men who served in it.

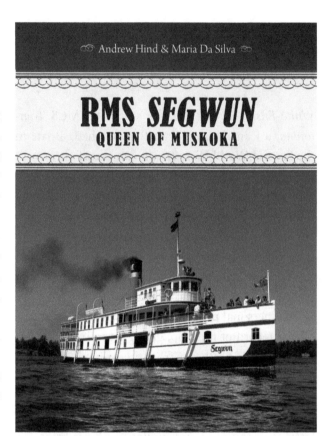